Are you interested in

 ☞ **W9-CUH-593**

a course management system that would

save you time & effort?

If the answer is *yes*, **CourseCompass is for you.**

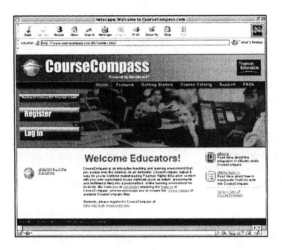

**Contact your local
Allyn & Bacon/Longman
sales representative**
for a free access code, or
visit www.coursecompass.com,
and take a tour of this course
management system.

**Technical support
is available for
faculty and students:**

support@coursecompass.com
1-800-677-6337

CourseCompass is an online course management system
designed to help you manage all the aspects of your course –
communication, information distribution, testing and grading.

Let it help you:

- **Communicate directly with your students** via email, discussion boards, and announcement pages.

- **Post documents for your course,** eliminating the need for course packs or handouts.

- **Administer online tests,** with automatic grading and analysis.

- **Provide your students with 24/7 access** to key course information, such as syllabus, assignments, and additional resources – as well as check his/her grade instantly.

Demo CourseCompass today! www.coursecompass.com

Best-Selling Professional Resources for College Instructors!

As the world's leader in education, Allyn & Bacon understands your interest in continual professional development. From the latest advancements in technology for the classroom to special insights for adjunct professors, these books were written for you! [See the Teaching Tips section at the back of the manual for teaching advice, ideas, and suggestions.]

Instructing and Mentoring the African American College Student: Strategies for Success in Higher Education
Louis B. Gallien, Jr., Regent University and
Marshalita Sims Peterson, Ph.D, Spelman College
©2005 / 0-205-38917-1

Grant Writing in Higher Education:
A Step-by-Step Guide
Kenneth Henson, The Citadel
©2004 / 0-205-38919-8

Using Technology in Learner-Centered Education:
Proven Strategies for Teaching and Learning
David G. Brown and Gordon McCray, both of Wake Forest University,
Craig Runde, Eckerd College and Heidi Schweizer, Marquette University
©2002 / 0-205-35580-3

Creating Learning-Centered Courses
for the World Wide Web
William B. Sanders, University of Hartford
©2001 / 0-205-31513-5

Success Strategies for Adjunct Faculty
Richard Lyons, Faculty Development Associates
©2004 / 0-205-36017-3

The Effective, Efficient Professor:
Teaching, Scholarship and Service
Philip C. Wankat, Purdue University
©2002 / 0-205-33711-2

Emblems of Quality in Higher Education:
Developing and Sustaining High-Quality Programs
Jennifer Grant Haworth, Loyola University, Chicago and
Clifton F. Conrad, University of Wisconsin, Madison,
©1997 / 0-205-19546-6

Faculty of Color in Academe: Bittersweet Success
Caroline Sotello Viernes Turner, Arizona State University
and Samuel L. Myers Jr., University of Minnesota
©2000 / 0-205-27849-3

An Introduction to Interactive Multimedia
Stephen J. Misovich, Jerome Katrichis, David Demers, William B. Sanders, all of the University of Hartford
©2003 / 0-205-34373-2

Learner-Centered Assessment on College Campuses:
Shifting the Focus from Teaching to Learning
Mary E. Huba, Iowa State University and Jann E. Freed, Central College
©2000 / 0-205-28738-7

The Online Teaching Guide: A Handbook of Attitudes, Strategies, and Techniques for the Virtual Classroom
Ken W. White and Bob H. Weight, both of University of Phoenix Online Faculty
©2000 / 0-205-29531-2

The Adjunct Professor's Guide to Success:
Surviving and Thriving in the College Classroom
Richard Lyons, Faculty Development Associates, Marcella L. Kysilka, and George E. Pawlas, both of University of Central Florida
©1999 / 0-205-28774-3

Teaching Tips for College and University Instructors: A Practical Guide
David Royse, University of Kentucky
©2001 / 0-205-29839-7

Advice for New Faculty Members
Robert Boice, Emeritus, SUNY Stony Brook
©2000 / 0-205-28159-1

Writing for Professional Publication:
Keys to Academic and Business Success
Kenneth Henson, The Citadel
©1999 / 0-205-28313-6

Teaching College in an Age of Accountability
Richard Lyons, Faculty Development Associates, Meggin McIntosh, University of Nevada - Reno, and Marcella L. Kysilka, University of Central Florida
©2003 / 0-205-35315-0

Save 20% on any of these resources when you order online...

www.ablongman.com/highered

Open-Book Testing: Why It Makes Sense

By Kay Burke, Ph.D.

Educators who allow students to take open-book tests are not teaching *for the test*; they are teaching *for understanding*. Most students agree that open-book tests are more challenging than traditional objective tests because they require high-order thinking skills rather than recall skills.

The greatest benefit from open-book testing may be that it encourages the type of thinking that will benefit students in the real world.

- Open-book tests focus on students learning important concepts rather than memorizing facts.

- They encourage students to utilize the lifelong learning skill of "accessing information" rather than memorizing data. In most jobs, people do not have to memorize formulas or discrete bits of data; they have to know how to find the important information they need in order to solve problems and complete projects.

- Open-book tests encourage students to highlight the text and organize their notes so they can find the information they need.

- Open-book tests encourage students to **apply** the information they have learned and **transfer** it to new situations, rather than just repeat the facts.

Sources:

Burke, K.B. *The mindful school: How to assess authentic learning*. Arlington Heights, IL. Skylight Professional Development.

Stiggins, R.J. (1985, October). *Improving assessment where it means the most: In the classroom*. Educational Leadership, pp. 69-74.

Wiggins, G. (1989, April). *Creating tests worth taking*. Educational Leadership, pp. 121-127

Wiggins, G., & McTighe, J. (1989). *Understanding by design*. Alexandria, VA: Association for Supervision and Curriculum Development.

Instructor's Manual and Test Bank

for

Parrillo

Strangers to These Shores
Race and Ethnic Relations
in the United States

Eighth Edition

prepared by

Jean Raniseski
Alvin Community College

Boston   New York   San Francisco
Mexico City   Montreal   Toronto   London   Madrid   Munich   Paris
Hong Kong   Singapore   Tokyo   Cape Town   Sydney

Copyright © 2006 Pearson Education, Inc.

All rights reserved. The contents, or parts thereof, may be reproduced with *Strangers to These Shores: Race and Ethnic Relations in the United States*, Eighth Edition, by Vincent N. Parrillo, provided such reproductions bear copyright notice, but may not be reproduced in any form for any other purpose without written permission from the copyright owner.

To obtain permission(s) to use the material from this work, please submit a written request to Allyn and Bacon, Permissions Department, 75 Arlington Street, Boston, MA 02116 or fax your request to 617-848-7320.

ISBN 0-205-45979-X

Printed in the United States of America

10 9 8 7 6 5 4 3 2 1   09 08 07 06 05

This work is protected by United States copyright laws and is provided solely for the use of instructors in teaching their courses and assessing student learning. Dissemination or sale of any part of this work (including on the World Wide Web) will destroy the integrity of the work and is not permitted. The work and materials from it should never be made available to students except by instructors using the accompanying text in their classes. All recipients of this work are expected to abide by these restrictions and to honor the intended pedagogical purposes and the needs of other instructors who rely on these materials.

Table of Contents

Instructor's Manual

Chapter 1: The Study of Minorities 1
Chapter 2: Culture and Social Structure 7
Chapter 3: Prejudice and Discrimination 14
Chapter 4: Dominant-Minority Relations 21
Chapter 5: Northern and Western Europeans 27
Chapter 6: Southern, Central, and Eastern Europeans 34
Chapter 7: The Native Americans 42
Chapter 8: East and Southeast Asian Americans 50
Chapter 9: Other Asian and Middle Eastern Americans 60
Chapter 10: Black Americans 67
Chapter 11: Hispanic Americans 76
Chapter 12: Religious Minorities 85
Chapter 13: Women as a Minority Group 93
Chapter 14: The Ever-Changing U.S. Mosaic 102

Test Bank   **112**

Chapter 1: The Study of Minorities 113
Chapter 2: Culture and Social Structure 121
Chapter 3: Prejudice and Discrimination 130
Chapter 4: Dominant-Minority Relations 138
Chapter 5: Northern and Western Europeans 146
Chapter 6: Southern, Central, and Eastern Europeans 154
Chapter 7: The Native Americans 162
Chapter 8: East and Southeast Asian Americans 170
Chapter 9: Other Asian and Middle Eastern Americans 178
Chapter 10: Black Americans 186
Chapter 11: Hispanic Americans 195
Chapter 12: Religious Minorities 203
Chapter 13: Women as a Minority Group 211
Chapter 14: The Ever-Changing U.S. Mosaic 219

Chapter 1

The Study of Minorities

Chapter 1 At-A-Glance

Detailed Outline	Instructor Resources	Print Supplements	Media Supplements	Professor Notes
The Stranger as a Social Phenomenon Similarity Attraction Social Distance Perceptions Interactions	**Lecture Topics:** Categorization of strangers. **Class Activity:** #1	**Test Bank Textbook Review Questions:** #1	**PowerPoint Media:** "America's Multicultural Heritage" (1995, Insight Media, 30 min.) "A Question of Race" (2001, Insight Media, 51 min.) **www.ablongman.com/parrillo**	
Sociological Perspective Functional Theory Conflict Theory Interactionist Theory	**Lecture Topics:** Dominant theoretical approaches to understand majority-minority relations.	**Test Bank Textbook Review Questions:** #4	**PowerPoint Media:** "Understanding Our Biases and Assumptions (Films for the Humanities & Sciences, 14 min.) **www.ablongman.com/parrillo**	
Minority Groups Development of a Definition Minority-Group Characteristics **Racial and Ethnic Groups**	**Lecture Topics:** Values, attitudes, customs, beliefs, and habits that are shared by social groups. Minority groups' characteristics. **Class Activities:** #2, 3	**Test Bank Textbook Review Questions:** # 2 & 5	**PowerPoint Media:** "Intercultural Communication" (1997, Insight Media, 30 min.) "Race and Ethnicity" (1991, Insight Media, 30 min.) "Is the Human Race Our Best Kept Secret?" (2002, Insight Media, 27 min.) **www.ablongman.com/parrillo**	

| Ethnocentrism Objectivity The Dillingham Flaw The Dynamics of Intergroup Relations | **Lecture Topics:** Preference for one's own culture, categorization, intergroup relations as dynamic social phenomenon. | **Test Bank International Scene Boxed Feature:** Enhancing German Interactions With Americans. **Textbook Review Questions:** #3 | **PowerPoint Media:** "Race: The World's Most Dangerous Myth" (1992, Insight Media, 60 min.) "Bugs for Breakfast: Food and Culture" (2001, Insight Media, 19 min.) **www.ablongman .com/parrillo** | |

CHAPTER 1

THE STUDY OF MINORITIES

LEARNING OBJECTIVES

1. To introduce students to the sociological perspective for the study of race and ethnic relations

2. To present the concept of the stranger as a social phenomenon as the focus through which to understand majority-minority interaction

3. To acquaint students with the basic concepts of minority groups, ethnocentrism, social behavior, social distance, and the difficulty of achieving objectivity

4. To present the concept of the Dillingham Flaw and its relevance to acceptance of diversity

SUMMARY

1. Numerous studies report that if people perceive strangers as similar to them, they are more attracted to them. This perception of similarity is more important than actual similarity. Social distance indices are an excellent measurement of similarity perceptions and social acceptance. The 2001 study found greater acceptance of diversity than ever before.

2. The initial response to strangers is categoric knowing, the generalization based on visual and possibly verbal input. Fear, suspicion, distrust, or resistance often replaces curiosity. While the native perceives the stranger in a very abstract, typified way, the stranger perceives the native in very concrete terms. For the stranger, the unfamiliar surroundings cannot be taken for granted, so everything is problematic.

3. Three major sociological perspectives shape analytical study of minorities. Functional theory emphasizes societal stability and interdependence, with dysfunctions seen as temporary maladjustments. Conflict theorists stress the inequalities maintained through false consciousness and exploitation. Interactionists focus on social interpretations and personal interaction patterns.

4. Minority groups share certain characteristics: 1) unequal treatment; 2) visibility; 3) group consciousness; 4) ascribed status; 5) endogamy. Women, though a minority group, do not fit the last category nor do the aged or handicapped fit the fourth.

5.   Race, subject to varying interpretations by social scientists, is based on biological considerations. Ethnicity refers to groups sharing a common cultural heritage based on national origin, language, religion, and/or other cultural attributes.

6.   Ethnocentrism, a normal tendency to prefer one's own way of doing things, is an important factor in understanding the response of a group of strangers. Eurocentrism and Afrocentrism are variations of ethnocentrism, with a biased focus on the history and cultural influences of either Western or African civilization.

7.   Because we are all products of our culture, objectivity in the study of race and ethnic relations is most difficult, if possible at all. Still, a conscientious effort to keep an open mind, to question all assumptions and opinions, is necessary.

8.   The Dillingham Flaw, its name inspired by the judgmental errors of a congressional commission (1907-1911), is any inaccurate comparison based on simplistic categorizations and anachronistic judgments. Its most common manifestation is in criticism of slow acculturation of today's immigrants as different from the Americanization of past immigrants.

9.   According to C. Wright Mills, ethnocentrism and subjectivity often prevent us from realizing that what appear to be simply personal troubles often transcend local settings and reflect instead structural changes and institutional contradictions.

10.   Intergroup relations continually change, as the result of migration, technology, war, economics, or attitudinal shifts. Throughout the world, even in recent years, numerous groups have gone through varying interaction patterns. Race and ethnic relations are a dynamic social phenomenon, about which we continually learn more.

11.   The International Scene boxed feature illustrates one effort to assist Germans in overcoming ethnocentric reactions to U.S. culture.

CLASS ACTIVITIES

1.   An effective first class session to promote interaction and to reveal the diversity of American society is to have each student give a brief autobiographical sketch of his/her background in national origin(s), religion(s), and number of generations the family has lived in the United States. The instructor can then build on this shared knowledge to speak about course objectives and how much the class is or is not a microcosm of the larger society, and what that means to the material to be studied.

2.   Drawing from local, state and federal statistics, determine the racial/ethnic composition of your area. How does this compare to your school's racial/ethnic composition? Why? How do the various groups in your area compare as to income, education, elected public office, unemployment, and other socioeconomic/political variables?

3.   Administer a social distance scale form (see Bogardus, 1928, 1958 for details). A simpler, less time-consuming approach would be to have students list their five closest friends on a sheet of paper. Once listed, have them sequentially identify the race, age, religion, and socioeconomic status of these five people. Answers should illustrate on personal terms the similarity-attraction concept.

INTERNET RESOURCES

At this book's Web site (http://www.ablongman.com/parrillo), students should select the cover icon, then Chapter 1 to find a variety of links, exercises, and activities pertinent to this content.

MEDIA MATERIALS

"America's Multicultural Heritage" (1995, Insight Media, 30 minutes)

Explores the mingling of cultural traditions that characterize the United States. It considers why certain groups came to the United States and looks at where particular ethnic groups settled. It stresses the importance of mutual respect and the principle of justice for all.

"A Question of Race" (2001, Insight Media, 51 minutes)

Questions whether race is an accurate biological identifier or a purely social construction. It presents real-life situations in which hidden cameras show adults and children encountering people of different races. Features commentary on the subtle reality of racial prejudice.

"Bugs for Breakfast: Food and Culture" (2001, Insight Media, 19 minutes)

This video presents a multicultural look at cultural eating habits, discussing why people eat and what they eat, and highlighting the food taboos of different cultures. It explores different eating patterns and reveals that acceptable food is not a question of taste, but culture.

"Intercultural communication" (1997, Insight Media, 30 minutes)

>   Explores the diversity of communication patterns among cultures, addresses cultural differences in verbal and nonverbal codes, and illustrates common barriers to effective intercultural communication.

"Is the Human Race Our Best Kept Secret?" (2002, Insight Media, 27 minutes)

>   Professor Joseph Graves of Arizona State University believes that humans cannot be separated by genetics into races. This program explores Graves' assertion that there are too many shared genes between people of European and African descent in the United States to allow for racial delineation.

"Race and Ethnicity" (1991, Insight Media, 30 minutes)

>   Explaining the sociological definition of minority, this program explores race, racism, ethnicity, the dynamics of prejudice and discrimination, and the theories of race and ethnic inequality.

"Race: The World's Most Dangerous Myth" (1992, Insight Media, 60 minutes)

>   Differentiates between social and biological definitions of race, genetic differences among races, including sickle cell anemia and lactose deficiency. Also considers how society and its institutions perpetuate racial stereotypes.

"Social Interaction in Diverse Settings" (1992, RMI Media Productions, 60 minutes)

>   Discussion of a social interaction model which provides students with a common basis for understanding groups and differences between groups.

"Understanding Our Biases and Assumptions" (Films for the Humanities & Sciences, 14 min.)

>   Explains the nature of biases and preconceptions, individual perspectives, and the role of peer groups, community institutions, schools, and the media in determining what is "good" and "bad." Members of minorities to speak out about how bias affects their lives, challenging viewers to examine their own biases and overcome them.

Chapter 2

Culture and Social Structure

Chapter 2 At-A- Glance

Detailed Outline	Instructor Resources	Print Supplements	Media Supplements	Professor Notes
The Concept of Culture The Reality Construct	**Lecture Topics:** Awareness and categorization of cultural differences and the role they play during social interactions. **Class Activities:** #1 & 2	**Test Bank** **Textbook Review** **Questions:** #1	**PowerPoint** **Media:** "Culture" (1991, Insight Media, 30 min.) **www.ablongman.com/ parrillo**	
Cultural Change Cultural Diffusion Subcultures	**Lecture Topics:** Borrowed elements of all cultures. Convergent and persistent subcultures.	**Test Bank** **Textbook Review** **Questions:** #2	**PowerPoint** **Media:** "Culture, Identity, and Behavior" (2003, Insight Media, 35 min.) "Degrees of Difference" (1999, PBS, 30 min.) "Everybody's Ethnic: Your Invisible Culture" (2001, Insight Media, 21 min.) **www.ablongman.com/ parrillo**	
Structural Conditions Stratification Social Class Class Consciousness Ethnicity and Social Class Blaming the Poor or Society	**Lecture Topics:** Interaction of ethnicity and social class. Basic U.S. Values. Blaming the poor. **Class Activities:** #3	**Test Bank** **Textbook Review** **Questions:** #3 & 4	**PowerPoint** **Media:** "Fatherless in America" (1994, Films for the Humanities & Sciences, 26 min.) "Social Class" (1991, Insight Media, 30 min.) "Children of Poverty" (1987, Films for the Humanities & Sciences, 26 min.) **www.ablongman.com/ parrillo**	

Intergroup Conflict Cultural Differentiation Structural Differentiation **Ethnic Stratification** The Power-Differential Theory The Internal-Colonialism Theory Origins of Ethnic Stratification	**Lecture Topics:** Exploitation of minority group members.	**Test Bank Textbook Review Questions: #4**	**PowerPoint Media:** "Intercultural Communication" (1997, Insight Media, 30 min.) "Understanding Cultural Differences" (1996, Insight Media, 30 min.) "A World of differences: Understanding Cross-Cultural Communication" (1997, University of California, 34 min.) **www.ablongman.com/ parrillo**	
Theories of Minority Integration Assimilation Theory Amalgamation Theory Accommoda-tion Theory **Is There a White Culture?**	**Lecture Topics:** Assimilation, Amalgamation, and Accommodation.	**Test Bank** International Scene: Attempts to Eliminate a Persistent Subculture. **Textbook Review Questions: #5 & 6**	**PowerPoint Media:** "White Identity Theory: Origins and Prospects" (1994, Insight Media, 60 min.) **www.ablongman.com/ parrillo**	

CHAPTER 2

CULTURE AND SOCIAL STRUCTURE

LEARNING OBJECTIVES

1. To develop student awareness of the differences in cultures and the role they play when people of different cultures interact

2. To provide students with an understanding of how the social structure affects intergroup relations

3. To examine the theoretical concepts and public expectations of how minorities should fit into the society

4. Overall, this chapter provides the context within which to study the various group experiences discussed in Chapters 5 to 13

SUMMARY

1. Culture consists of the values, attitudes, customs, beliefs, and habits that are shared by members of a society. It provides the screen through which we perceive the world around us.

2. Humans respond not to stimuli, but to their definition of stimuli. According to the Thomas Theorem, this factor can result in a false perception becoming an actuality through action. Through cultural transmission the definitions are passed on to the next generation.

3. About 90 percent of the elements of all cultures (except for remote and isolated societies) are borrowed through cultural diffusion. Change also occurs through contact, after which many interaction patterns are possible between two groups.

4. Immigrants usually follow a chain migration pattern, settling in an area already containing family, friends, or compatriots. There an ethnic community evolves, with parallel social institutions helping promote cohesiveness and insulation from the alien host society.

5. Convergent subcultures go through a transitional stage and their members usually experience the problems of marginality. Persistent subcultures are more insulated but they may encounter problems with the dominant society because they do not assimilate.

6. Structural conditions are also important influences in intergroup relations. The economy and chances for upward mobility, differences between the sending and host countries, and accessibility to one's homeland or compatriots—all affect the interaction patterns.

7. Ethnicity and social class are heavily intertwined. What passes for ethnic observations are often recognizable characteristics of class position in society.

8. Social stratification, ranging from rigid to flexible and subtle, influences how groups perceive one another. The culture-of-poverty hypothesis places blame upon the poor for continuing their situation from one generation to the next through transmission of subcultural values. A variation on the culture of poverty theme is Moynihan's linkage of cultural value deficiencies and family disintegration among African Americans. Social scientists, however, have been unable to find evidence supporting this view. Perhaps the "value-stretch" view of lower-class adoption of more realistic values to meet lower expectations, while not renouncing prevailing values, is closer to the mark.

9. Differences in culture, particularly religion or visible features (clothing, skin color, or behavior) may cause conflict. More likely causes for intergroup conflict are social class antagonisms, competition for scarce resources, and societal conditions (e.g., the economy).

10. Two mid-range conflict analyses offer insight into exploitation of minority groups. Lieberson's power differential theory suggests resulting conflict or assimilation depends on the power relationship between the indigenous and migrant groups. Blauner's internal colonialism theory points to failure to gain economic and political control of their internal communities as the reason for permanent black ghettos.

11. Although most Americans give lip service to the romantic but false notion of a melting pot, in reality many want others to assimilate (Anglo-conformity). Assimilation has several aspects or subprocesses, chiefly cultural, marital, and structural. Some observers suggest the existence of a triple melting pot, with the emergence of three major faiths and multi-generational decline of ethnicity. In recent years, pluralism, which existed long before its emergence as a theoretical concept, has become more widely accepted. Moreover, assimilation and pluralism have always coexisted; they are not mutually exclusive.

12. Advocates of the concept of a white culture independent of "American" culture suggest our recognition of its existence is a necessary first step to build a truly multiracial society.

13. The International Scene boxed feature discusses the Kurds as a persistent subculture in Iran, Iraq, and Turkey.

CLASS ACTIVITIES

1. To help students understand more fully the difficulty in coping with a different culture, administer the Chitlin' or BITCH tests under mock I.Q. testing conditions. Even young, inner city blacks will fare poorly on many questions. Serves as object lesson and discussion base about cultural bias, evaluation instruments, and outgroup perceptions.

2. BAFA BAFA: a cross-culture simulation game for an entire class. Gives participants experience in observing and interacting with a different culture. Works very well. (Social Studies School Service, Culver City, California)

3. Play "Carefully Taught," the Rodgers and Hammerstein song quoted in this chapter. Lines such as "before it's too late," open up good question-answer dialog possibilities. Similarly, Kris Kristofferson's "Jesus was a Capricorn" offers an excellent means for discussing ethnocentrism with lines such as, "Everybody's got to have somebody to look down on."

INTERNET RESOURCES

At this book's Web site (http://www.ablongman.com/parrillo), students should select the cover icon, then Chapter 2 to find a variety of links, exercises, and activities pertinent to this content.

MEDIA MATERIALS

"A World of Differences: Understanding Cross-Cultural Communication" (1997, University of California, 34 minutes)

Examines 14 key facets of cross-cultural miscommunication, exploring the power and subtlety of cultural differences. Examples include personal space, touching, gestures, etiquette and ritual, expression of emotions, ideas about edible food, courtship patterns.

"America's Multicultural Heritage" (1995, Insight Media, 30 minutes)

This program explores the mingling of cultural traditions that characterizes the United States. It considers why certain groups came to the United States and looks at where particular ethnic groups settled. It stresses the importance of mutual respect and the principle of justice for all.

"Children of Poverty" (1987, Films for the Humanities & Sciences, 26 minutes)

Profiles U.S. children living in poverty in female-headed households, and the problems of mothers trying to find shelter and food to survive, prevent kids from becoming crime victims or criminals and to nurture their self-esteem.

"Culture" (1991 video, Insight Media, 30 minutes)

Portrays cultural diversity in the United States, the development of culture, and the role of language. Profiles Louisiana Cajun, Cherokee, and Chinese settlements in the South and how these subcultures address human needs.

"Culture, Identity, and Behavior" (2003, Insight Media, 35 minutes)

In this program, experts explore the interrelationships among culture, identity, and behavior, and evaluate models proposed by Freud, Sapir, Benedict, Meade, and others. It looks at how culture, social structure, belief systems, and altered states affect social behavior, self-actualization, and deviance. It also compares how major cultures view life cycle events, tattoos, and morality.

"Degrees of Difference: Culture Matters on Campus" (1999, PBS, 30 minutes)

Understanding differences on campus is framed as an ongoing experience rather than a series of isolated events. The program is divided into five segments that can be watched together to promote general discussion, or watched individually to facilitate discussion about specific issues.

"Fatherless in America" (1994, Films for the Humanities & Sciences, 26 minutes)

Because of divorce, single-parenthood, incarceration, and welfare rules—nearly 40 percent of American children sleep in homes where their father does not live. This program looks at the problem, its causes, and its effects, from poverty to violence. It also looks at some efforts to reverse the growing trend toward fatherlessness in America.

"Intercultural Communication" (1997, Insight Media, 30 minutes)

Explores the diversity of communication patterns among cultures, addresses cultural differences in verbal and nonverbal codes, and illustrates common barriers to effective intercultural communication.

"Race and Ethnicity" (2002, Insight Media, 30 minutes)

This video explains how race and ethnicity influence social patterns of human interaction. Using real life examples, it considers such problems as racism, prejudice, discrimination, segregation, and genocide.

"Social Class" (1991, Insight Media, 30 minutes)

Is social stratification in the United States inherently discriminatory? This video shows how social class determines the lifestyles, world views, and opportunities of two teenaged girls. The program also covers such issues as social mobility, poverty, perceptions of social class, and the measurement of social inequality.

"Understanding Cultural Differences" (1996, Insight Media, 30 minutes)

To deepen the viewer's understanding of other cultures, this video interviews students of different cultures and ethnic backgrounds to explore diverse traditions and views. Stresses the importance of overcoming barriers and dealing with a multicultural environment.

"White Identity Theory: Origins and Prospects" (1994, Insight Media, 60 minutes)

Rita Hardiman, the originator of white identity theory, discusses how white people often forget that they have a culture. She considers racism as a white problem and describes the stages of white identity development.

Chapter 3

Prejudice and Discrimination

Chapter 3 At-A-Glance

Detailed Outline	Instructor Resources	Print Supplements	Media Supplements	Professor Notes
Prejudice Psychology of Prejudice Sociology of Prejudice Stereotyping Television's Influence Advertising and Music Can Prejudice Be Reduced?	**Lecture Topics:** Understanding of the nature of prejudice, increase awareness of the dangers of stereotyping, possible causes of stereotyping and prejudice, role of ethnic humor and the media in perpetuating prejudice, and explore the possible causes of prejudice and their elimination. **The Ethnic Experience:** Reducing Prejudice Through the Jigsaw Method **The Ethnic Experience:** Impact of the Media **Class Activities:** #1, 2 & 3	**Test Bank Review Questions: #1 & 2**	PowerPoint Presentation "Can You See the Color Gray?" (1997, University of California, 54 min.) "The Distorted Image: Stereotype and Caricature in American Popular Graphics, 1850-1922" (60 slides w/cassette or record, Anti-Defamation League, 30 min.) "Prejudice: Eye of the Storm" (1981, Insight Media, 25 min.) "Understanding Prejudice" (1996, Films for the Humanities and Sciences, 50 min.) **www.ablongman.com/ parrillo**	

Discrimination	Lecture Topic:	Test Bank	PowerPoint	
Levels of Discrimination Relationships Between Prejudice and Discrimination Social and Institutional Discrimination Affirmative Action Controversy	Develop student understanding of the different aspects of discrimination and examine the complex interrelationships between prejudice and discrimination. **The International Scene:** Discrimination in Northern Ireland		**Media:** "Affirmative Action Under Fire: When Is It Reverse Discrimination?" "Beyond Black and White: Affirmative Action in America" (1999, Films for the Humanities and Sciences, 58 min.) "Prejudice, Discrimination, and Stereotypes" (1993, Insight Media, 22 min.) "Race and Ethnicity" (1991, RMI Media Productions, Inc., 30 min.) "Racial Profiling and Law Enforcement: America in Black and White" (1998, Films for the Humanities and Sciences, 41 min.) **www.ablongman.com/ parrillo**	

CHAPTER 3

PREJUDICE AND DISCRIMINATION

LEARNING OBJECTIVES

1. To develop student understanding of the nature of prejudice

2. To increase student awareness of the dangers of stereotyping, and its perpetuation through ethnic humor and the media

3. To explore the possible causes of prejudice and their elimination

4. To develop student understanding of the different aspects of discrimination

5. To examine the complex interrelationships between prejudice and discrimination

SUMMARY

1. Prejudice is a system of negative beliefs, feelings, and action-orientations regarding a certain group or groups of people.

2. The psychology of prejudice examines the subjective state of individuals, noting three levels of prejudice: cognitive, emotional, and action-orientation. Some possible causes are self-justification, personality, and frustration aggression.

3. The sociology of prejudice examines the objective conditions of society as social forces behind prejudiced attitudes. Some possible causes are socialization, competition, and conformity to social norms.

4. A stereotype is an oversimplified generalization by which we attribute certain traits or characteristics to any person in a group without regard to individual differences. Once established, stereotypes are difficult to eradicate, as several studies have shown.

5. Ethnophaulisms are derogatory words or expressions used to describe racial or ethnic groups. Ethnic humor is often at the expense of a particular group, but may also serve to strengthen group cohesiveness, dissociate oneself from stereotypes of one's group, or affirm oneself by pointing out the absurdity of one's predicaments.

6.   Television plays a major role in shaping attitudes and perceptions. Studies find television usually perpetuates stereotypes as well as reaffirming viewer attitudes. One study showed one-fourth of respondents believed TV depicted reality and influenced their racial and ethnic attitudes.

7.   Greater interaction and education do not necessarily reduce the level of prejudice in a society. Use of cooperative learning techniques in a classroom setting has demonstrated an effective means of promoting better intergroup understanding and self-esteem.

8.   Discrimination is an action or practice of differential and unequal treatment of other groups of people, usually along racial, religious, or ethnic lines. Like prejudice, discrimination also exists at different levels of intensity: verbal expression, avoidance, exclusion, physical abuse, and extermination. Ethnoviolence is a new term describing a wide range of behavior against a particular group. Merton explains how social-situational variables can influence the relationship between prejudice and discrimination.

9.   The International Scene boxed feature discusses institutional discrimination against the Irish in Northern Ireland.

10.   From its origins in 1941 through the present, affirmative action programs have been controversial. Supreme Court rulings in the late 1970s and 1980s upheld the principle of affirmative action but since 1989, a more conservative court has been ruling against "race-conscious remedies." Evidence about the program's success is mixed. Minority group opponents call affirmative action "misplaced condescension" that has poisoned race relations. Negative public opinion polls and proposed legislation suggest the real possibility of significant changes to come.

CLASS ACTIVITIES

1.   Check the school and public libraries for a collection of jokes and humorous stories. How many stereotypes of minorities are in such books? What roles do humorous images of minority groups play in our perceptions and thinking?

2.   Have students do a content analysis of network television programs for their depiction of minority group members.

3.   Through a replication of the Princeton study of stereotyping among undergraduates or in class discussion, evoke from students their thoughts about the stereotypes of minority or dominant groups with which they have grown up. What do they think about how such stereotypes emerged in their upbringing?

INTERNET RESOURCES

At this book's Web site (http://www.ablongman.com/parrillo), students should select the cover icon, then Chapter 3 to find a variety of links, exercises, and activities pertinent to this content.

MEDIA MATERIALS

"Affirmative Action Under Fire: When Is It Reverse Discrimination?" (1997, Films for the Humanities & Sciences, 22 minutes)

Reviews the reverse discrimination complaint lodged by a white female high school teacher in New Jersey, when she was laid off instead of an African American with equal tenure and equivalent credentials. By 1995, it became a national issue of great political and legal significance, leading to a surprising out-of-court settlement funded by civil rights groups.

"Attitudes" (2001, Insight Media, 34 minutes)

Examining how attitudes are formed, this video explains cognitive dissonance and in-group/out-group relations. It considers stereotyping and ethnocentrism, discusses the Sheriff Robbers Cave experiment on combating group prejudice, and identifies a three-step process for overcoming prejudice.

"Beyond Black and White: Affirmative Action in America" (1999, Films for the Humanities & Sciences, 58 minutes)

All sides of the affirmative action issue seek an end to racism of all types. But do opportunities for some have to come at the expense of others? In this Fred Friendly Seminar, a what-if scenario revolves around a university's efforts to enroll a diverse student body of qualified candidates. Panelists include advocates and opponents of affirmative action, and policy activists from racial and ethnic communities.

"Can You See the Color Gray?" (1997, University of California, 54 minutes)

This unusual documentary, which can also be shown in two or four segments, is sure to provoke discussion and self-reflection about racial differences and stereotypes. It shows numerous people from diverse racial and ethnic backgrounds as they grapple with probing questions about their racial attitudes and their feelings about their own ethnicity.

"The College Eye: The Angry Eye" (2001, Insight Media, 35 minutes)

> Jane Elliott describes this version of her seminal blue-eyed/brown-eyed experiment set in a college environment, as "an injection of the live virus of racism." Designed to address issues of diversity and prejudice in both educational and corporate settings, the program shows young adults from various ethnic and racial backgrounds as they are forced to explore racism in contemporary American society.

Dealing With Racism and Hate (2002, Insight Media, 34 minutes)

> While some forms of racism and hate are more obvious than others, most individuals will at least once be a victim of judgment as a result of their appearance, ethnicity, occupation, or sexual preference. This program explores the different types of racism and hate and investigates ways to combat them.

"The Distorted Image: Stereotype and Caricature in American Popular Graphics, 1850-1922" (60 slides w/cassette or record, Anti-Defamation League, 30 minutes)

> Media cartoons and illustrations reveal the extent and nature of stereotyping which has affected all U.S. minority groups, with particular emphasis on stereotypes of Blacks, Chinese, Jewish, and Irish.

"Prejudice: Eye of the Storm" (1981, Insight Media, 25 minutes)

> A classic study on how wholesome 3rd graders can be infected with the ugly virus of discrimination as the class is divided into "blue eyes" and brown eyes." Each group experiences discrimination by the other on alternating days.

"Prejudice, Discrimination, and Stereotypes" (1993, Insight Media, 22 minutes)

> Looks at the roots of prejudice and discrimination and their effects on both the victim and perpetrator. Viewers learn how to avoid stereotyping and how to promote tolerance and respect for others.

"Race and Ethnicity" (1991, RMI Media Productions, 30 minutes)

> Shows the difference between prejudice, discrimination and racism using historical and current examples. Explores the effects of prejudice and discrimination through the eyes of Asian, Hispanic and African-American families.

"Racial Profiling and Law Enforcement: America in Black and White" (1998, Films for the Humanities & Sciences, 41 minutes)

> DWB: Driving While Black. For many African-Americans, simply having dark skin seems to be grounds for being pulled over on the highway and searched for drugs. Police call it "profiling," based on years of successful drug interdiction through traffic stops, but angry and humiliated victims call it "racial profiling" want it stopped. In part one of this program, ABC News anchor Ted Koppel investigates the issue from the victims' points of view, with special commentary by law professor and former OJ Simpson prosecutor Christopher Darden. Some language may be objectionable.

"Understanding Prejudice" (1996, Films for the Humanities & Sciences, 50 minutes)

> Discusses the history and nature of prejudice and its effects and asks: Where does prejudice come from? Why does it exist? Where are we headed as a society? Interviews illuminate different kinds of prejudices and stereotypes.

Chapter 4
Dominant-Minority Relations

Chapter 4 At-A-Glance

Detailed Outline	Instructor Resources	Print Supplements	Media Supplements	Professor Notes
Minority-Group Responses Ethnic- and Racial-Group Identity Avoidance Deviance Defiance Acceptance	**Lecture Topics:** Examine minority response patterns to prejudice and discrimination	**Test Bank Textbook Review Questions: #1 & 2**	**PowerPoint Media:** "Deviance" (1991, Insight Media, 30 min.) **www.ablongman.com/parrillo**	
Consequences of Minority-Group Status Negative Self-Image The Vicious Circle Marginality Middleman Minorities	**Learning Objectives:** Ethnic identity, personal shame and passivity. **Class Activities:** #1	**Test Bank Textbook Review Questions: #3 & 4**	**PowerPoint Media:** "Social Interaction Model" (2001 Insight Media, 60 min.) **www.ablongman.com/parrillo**	
Dominant-Group Responses Legislative Controls Segregation Expulsion Xenophobia Annihilation Hate Groups and Hate Crimes	**Lecture Topics:** Relevant legislation, segregation issues, deportation, fear, genocide, lynchings, and motivation for hate crimes, **Class Activities:** #2 & 3	**Test Bank International Scene:** Xenophobia in Germany	**PowerPoint Media:** "Affirmative Action: The History of an Idea" (1996, Films for the Humanities & Sciences, 58 min.) "Divided We Stand" (1996, Films for the Humanities & Sciences, 49 min.) "Dealing With Diversity: Hate Groups in the U.S.A.." (1992, RMI Media Productions, 60 min.) "Skinheads U.S.A.: The Pathology of Hate" (1993, Films for the Humanities & Sciences, 54 min.) **www.ablongman.com/parrillo**	

| Exploitation | Lecture Topics: Exploitation by other minority group members and/or by majority group members. | Test Bank Textbook Review Questions: #5 | PowerPoint Media: "Aggression, Bullying, and Intimidation" (2001, Insight Media, 28 min.) **www.ablongman.com/parrillo** | |

CHAPTER 4

DOMINANT-MINORITY RELATIONS

LEARNING OBJECTIVES

1. To examine minority response patterns to prejudice and discrimination

2. To develop student understanding of the concepts of negative self-image, the vicious circle, marginality, and middleman minorities

3. To examine dominant response patterns to minority groups

4. To introduce three middle-range conflict theories about minority group exploitation

SUMMARY

1. Groups not part of the societal mainstream typically develop their own group identity based on ethnic (cultural or national) ties or race. Ethnic-group identity endures through resilient ethnic communities, minority media, and socialization. It can be especially protracted on the basis of religion, whether among persistent subcultures or large groups of recent arrivals. Racial-group identity provides ingroup bonding that satisfies the need for belonging, helps develop a sense of pride, and serves as a buttress against racism. Group identity can have either positive or negative consequences, and is thus an important social phenomenon in the study of race and ethnic relations.

2. Although personality characteristics play an important role in determining how individuals respond to unfavorable conditions, minority groups tend to respond mainly in four behavioral patterns. Avoidance may take the form of emigration or withdrawal from societal interaction. Deviance, usually engaged in only by a small segment, nevertheless results in negative stereotyping of the entire group; it can range from heavy drinking and brawling to drugs and crime. Defiance is an open challenge to unequal treatment, while acceptance of the situation can be stoic, resentful submission, or conscious role-playing.

3. Negative self-image is a fairly general tendency among minority-group members, causing a sense of personal shame or passivity. A vicious circle, or cumulative causation, intensifies negative reactions through negative expectations. Marginality occurs when minority-group members are caught between their own identity and values and those of the dominant culture. Children of immigrants often experience marginality more, though a strong emotional support system within the ethnic subcommunity may insulate against any negative effects.

4.   Middleman minorities exist in many dominant-subordinate stratification systems. Serving as an intermediate buffer between the top and bottom strata, such minorities perform mediating commerce links between the two, remaining either temporarily or indefinitely in that role.

5.   In addition to favorable or indifferent actions, dominant groups may enact legislation to restrict immigration of particular groups or to deny them political power or educational opportunities. Spatial or social segregation also confines a group's full participation in society. Xenophobia, the irrational fear of foreigners, often results in such drastic measures as expulsion or annihilation.

6.   The International Scene boxed feature discusses neo-Nazi violence against foreigners and voter xenophobia in Germany.

7.   In 2003, a total of 751 hate groups were active. About one-fifth are the KKK (158), then neo-Nazis (149), and black separatist groups (136), including the Nation of Islam. Other hate groups were neo-Confederates (91); followed by racist skinheads (39), and then 31 Christian Identity groups. Georgia contains the largest number of hate groups (54), followed by Texas (53), California and South Carolina (45), Florida (39), North Carolina and Ohio (33), New Jersey (30), Pennsylvania (29), Tennessee (28), Mississippi (27), Louisiana (26), Virginia (25), and Alabama and New York (24). Hate crime offenses—only some committed by members of organized hate groups—numbered over 9,300 in 1998, involving over 9,800 victims. Motivations were racial bias (61 percent), religious bias (16 percent), sexual orientation bias (13 percent), or ethnic bias (10 percent). Despite more severe punishment in most states for hate crimes, and the additional possibility of federal prosecution, the rise in hate groups and hate crimes continues.

8.   Exploitation of minority groups, sometimes by some of their own group members, has historically been a worldwide problem. Bonacich's split labor market theory sees prejudice and labor conflict occurring when differential wage levels spark ethnic antagonism.

CLASS ACTIVITIES

1.   Divide the class into small working groups. Give each group a different racial/ethnic group about which to apply the vicious circle phenomenon. Have them report out their models.

2.   Using your college student center and the entire campus as a microcosm of society, have students identify places/instances of social and spatial segregation (e.g., proprietary claims to cafeteria tables by various campus groups, free-period hangouts, etc.).

3.   A guest speaker from your local historical society could speak to the class about depiction of past minority groups in your regional newspapers.

INTERNET RESOURCES

At this book's Web site (http://www.ablongman.com/parrillo), students should select the cover icon, then Chapter 4 to find a variety of links, exercises, and activities pertinent to this content.

MEDIA MATERIALS

"Affirmative Action: The History of an Idea" (1996, Films for the Humanities & Sciences, 58 minutes)

Using archival footage and interviews with scholars, this program explores the historical roots of affirmative action and the current debate over its usefulness, looking at the University of California, Berkeley, struggling with how to maintain diversity without minority preferences, and at Chicago, under challenge for its hiring/promotion policies.

"Aggression, Bullying, and Intimidation" (2001, Insight Media, 28 minutes)

Investigating the root causes of aggressive behavior, this video examines its increasing prevalence in U.S. society. It discusses the underlying reasons some individuals adopt belligerent attitudes; shows how these attitudes can trigger inappropriate confrontations; and teaches strategies for avoiding and diffusing incendiary situations.

"Dealing With Diversity: Hate Groups in the U.S.A." (1992, RMI Media Productions, 60 min.)

Examines the distribution and types of hate groups, and the case for white supremacy. Includes interview with Arthur Jones of the America First Committee.

"Deviance" (1991, Insight Media, 30 minutes)

Showing the continuum of deviance from minor cultural variations to destructive behaviors, this program analyzes deviance as a social, historical, and cultural reality that embraces a wide range of behavior. It examines the dimensions of deviance and deviant subcultures and provides various sociological explanations.

"Divided We Stand" (1996, Films for the Humanities & Sciences, 49 minutes)

> Examines the divisive use of genetic studies to prove racial superiority. A sociologist uses low black IQ test scores to justify welfare cuts. An Afrocentrist says melanin stimulates black intellectual and artistic abilities. An expert explains why studies report black children walk and talk earlier than white children and cope better with noise, and another expert gives DNA evidence disputing major racial differences.

"Skinheads USA: The Pathology of Hate" (1993, Films for the Humanities & Sciences, 54 minutes)

> Gives an inside look at a neo-Nazi Skinhead organization, its operations, its personalities, the group's daily activities at its headquarters, White Power rallies and recruitment drives, and even visits inside a prison, where four Skinheads are jailed following the murder of a black man. Powerfully captures firsthand the distorted idealism and openly racist objectives of the neo-Nazi youth movement. (Note: Contains profanity and violence. Preview first.)

"Social Interaction Model" (2001, Insight Media, 60 minutes)

> A social interaction model clarifies the dynamics and implications of human social behavior. This video presents a social interaction model designed to elucidate the way people interact in culturally diverse settings. It focuses on the five major components of the model and shows how they overlap.

Chapter 5

Northern and Western Europeans

Chapter 5 At-A-Glance

Detailed Outline	Instructor Resources	Print Supplements	Media Supplements	Professor Notes
Sociohistorical Perspective Colonial Period Early National Period Pre-Civil War Period Structural Conditions	**Lecture Topics:** U.S. white ethnic experience from colonial beginnings to the Civil War. **Class Activities:** #1	**Test Bank Textbook Review Questions:** #1	**PowerPoint Media:** "A Nation of Immigrants" (1967, Anti-Defamation League, 52 min.) "Immigration, Social Policy, and Employment" (2001, Insight Media, 60 min.) www.ablongman.com/parrillo	
The English The Dutch The French The Germans The Irish The Scandinavians and Finns The Scots The Welsh	**Lecture Topic:** Push and pull factors associated with each group's immigration, how these strangers adjusted to a new society, cultural diversity in their homeland and the new world.	**Test Bank The Ethnic Experience:** Health Inspection at Ellis Island. Immigrant Expectations **Textbook Review Questions:** #4	**PowerPoint Media:** "Celtic Waves: The Flow of Irish Immigration" (2002, Insight Media, 54 min.) "Ellis Island" (1997, Insight Media, 150 min.) "The German Americans" (2000, PBS, 57 min). "'May the Road Rise to Meet You': The Irish American Experience" (1997, PBS, 57 min.) www.ablongman.com/parrillo	
Social Realities for Women	**Lecture Topics:** Women's rights in the new world.	**Test Bank**	**PowerPoint** www.ablongman.com/parrillo	

Northern and Western European Assimilation	**Lecture Topics:** Assimilation, Amalgamation and Accommodation in the new world, who adjusted easiest to the new environment and culture? **Class Activities:** #2	**Test Bank International Scene:** Britain's Approach Toward Ethnic Minorities **Textbook Review Questions:** #2, 3	**PowerPoint Media:** "Creole and Mixed Ethnic Americans" (2001, Insight Media, 60 min.) "What Does It Mean to Be White? The Invisible Whiteness of Being" (2004, Insight Media, 60 min.) **www.ablongman.com/parrillo**	
Sociological Analysis Functionalist View Conflict View Interactionist View	**Lecture Topics:** compare and contrast the three main theoretical views of immigration and acculturation.	**Test Bank Textbook Review Questions:** #5	**PowerPoint www.ablongman.com/parrillo**	

CHAPTER 5

NORTHERN AND WESTERN EUROPEANS

LEARNING OBJECTIVES

1. To examine, from a sociohistorical perspective, U.S. white ethnic experience from colonial beginnings to the Civil War

2. To show early majority-minority interaction patterns that still continue among other racial and ethnic groups

3. To study specifically the English, Dutch, French, Germans, Irish, Scandinavians, Scots, and Welsh as strangers adjusting to a new society.

SUMMARY

1. From the time of the first settlements, cultural diversity existed among different nationalities, among the thirteen English colonies, and between Native Americans and Europeans. Religion was often a source of social conflict in pre-Revolutionary times. Expulsion, avoidance, annihilation, and spatial segregation were all evident in this period.

2. In the early national period, English influence was extensive in language, religion, law, educational and governmental institutions, and cultural heritage. Separation of the church and state, as stipulated in the First Amendment, provided a more hospitable environment for religious minorities, but Quakers, Mormons, Catholics, Jews, and others suffered prejudice and discrimination nonetheless.

3. Anglo-Saxon influence and fierce nationalism resulted in xenophobia, particularly in relation to the French and Irish. Federalists looked upon the Republican movement as an evil of the foreign-born population. The Alien and Sedition Acts of 1798 illustrate a dominant group's legislative efforts to enforce rigid social control over a minority.

4. Irish, German, and other immigrants entered a country between 1820 and 1860 that was more stable and interdependent and had a more common culture than the colonists had found. When they attempted to fit into an established society, Irish and German Catholics and Jews encountered great resistance and active nativist movements against them.

5.   Early English settlers, as strangers in a strange land, experienced the same culture shock that later immigrants from other countries did.   Nineteenth-century English artisans, mill hands, and miners had the advantage of possessing needed job skills in a land of English heritage. Despite encountering little discrimination, many British immigrants returned home because they found the United States less "civilized" than they expected.

6.   The International Scene box explains how the British fight discrimination and racial inequality through encouraging workplace inclusiveness rather than using government mandates which create a backlash of resentment.

7.   Pluralism marked the Dutch experience both in their tolerance of other groups when they controlled New Netherland and in their persistence as a subculture for many generations after English domination. Mid-nineteenth century Dutch religious refugees settled in the Midwest in ethnic clusters.

8.   More Germans have come to the United States than any other nationality. In Pennsylvania Colony the presence of a large German subculture led to concern by some Americans that the German language and culture would be retained. Nineteenth-century German immigrants were quite diverse, settling in agrarian communities in the Midwest and in subcommunities in many eastern and Midwestern cities. The nativist movement of the 1850s and the Americanization movement of the World War I era mark two efforts by the dominant society to suppress the Germans in the United States.

9.   Protestant English Americans disliked the Irish for their religion, peasant culture, and anti-British feelings. Blatant discrimination in hiring and housing, in nativist movements, and in mob violence reflected this hostility. Irish drinking, brawling, or aggressive reactions only reinforced the negative stereotype, so the Irish turned inward, particularly in their practice of endogamy. The Civil War and influx of southern and eastern Europeans helped to ease the antipathy toward the Irish. Their command of English, their entrance into public service positions, and the gaining of political power in the cities-all aided their upward mobility. High unemployment in Ireland in the 1980s prompted massive emigration to the United States, about 32,000 legal immigrants and perhaps 50,000 illegals. Since the 1990s, greatly improved economic conditions in Ireland and a low birth rate reduced emigration to the United States to less than 1,000 annually.

10.   *Scandinavian* became a term used by Norwegians, Swedes, and Danes themselves to avoid mistaken labeling by outsiders. Settling primarily in the northern Midwest, they each formed separate ethnic communities, which have retained their cultural traditions, in some measures, to the present time.

11.   Scots were a sizable minority in the formative years of the nation, but the greatest number came as working-class immigrants during the period of industrial expansion (1871-1930).

12.   The Welsh were a distinct minority, mostly farmers and miners, who established ethnic communities in New York, Pennsylvania, Ohio and Illinois.

13.   Functional analysis emphasizes the economic opportunity afforded immigrants as they forged a civilization in a vast, rich, undeveloped country. Dysfunctions created by the arrival of many newcomers eventually ended as society adjusted and assimilation occurred.

14.   Conflict theorists stress Anglo-American domination, the Federalist elite resisting "common" newcomers, and economic exploitation of immigrants, particularly the Irish.

15.   Interactionists focus on how differing social interpretations by the Dutch, Quakers, and Puritans resulted in different responses to the newcomers. Also, Protestant Americans saw German Jews and Irish Catholics as a threat to the "American" way of life, which led to bitter conflict.

CLASS ACTIVITIES

1.   A guest speaker from an ethnic club for northern and western Europeans (such as the Ancient Order of Hiberians or a *Songerbund)* could tell the class about the history and purpose of that organization in promoting their cultural heritage.

2.   Discuss the settlement of northern and western Europeans in your area. Do current local statistics reflect migration of European descendants or geographic longevity? What factors do students think contribute to this pattern?

INTERNET RESOURCES

At this book's Web site (http://www.ablongman.com/parrillo), students should select the cover icon, then Chapter 5 to find a variety of links, exercises, and activities pertinent to this content.

MEDIA MATERIALS

"A Nation of Immigrants" (1967, Anti-Defamation League, 52 minutes)

Depicts immigration to the United States from colonial times to mid-1960s, contrasting immigrant dreams and hopes with the hate-mongering and bigotry which faced them. Based on the book by President Kennedy, the film is narrated by Richard Basehart with an introduction by Robert F. Kennedy.

"Celtic Waves: The Flow of Irish Immigration" (2002, Insight Media, 54 minutes)

This program explores the effects of 150 years of emigration trends on the culture of Ireland. It examines four periods: the 1840s famine, the turn of the 20th century, the hostile 1950s, and the emergence of the "Celtic tiger" economy in the 1980s and 1990s. The program features interviews with the economists and historians who examine the Sociopolitical, economic, and psychological transformation of Irish society and culture.

"Creole and Mixed Ethnic Americans" (2001, Insight Media, 60 minutes)

Describing the origins of Creole culture in New Orleans and the subsequent impact of this culture on the United States, this video examines the phenomenon of ethnic mixing. It discusses ideas about the significance of ethnicity and considers some of the issues that can affect mixed-race couples.

"Ellis Island" (1997, Insight Media, 150 minutes)

With oral histories, photographs, films, and dramatic re-creations, this set tells the story of Ellis Island. It shows the process – including days of waiting, lice inspections, and physical examinations – millions of people endured before they were allowed entry into the United States.

"The German Americans" (2000, PBS, 57 minutes)

Explores the German-American experience and celebrates the cultural ties that still bond generations after 400 years in the United States. Also highlights German Americans who embodied the spirit of the German work ethic and philosophy and became American icons, such as President Eisenhower, Babe Ruth, Lawrence Welk, and Charles Schulz.

"Immigration, Social Policy, and Employment" (2001, Insight Media, 60 minutes)

In this video, students discuss the history of immigration law in the United States. The program examines the successive waves of immigrants, addresses the reasons people chose to move to the United States, and explores their contributions to American culture. It closes with an examination of the impact of growing diversity on the current and future workforce.

"'May the Road Rise to Meet You': The Irish-American Experience" (1997, PBS, 57 minutes)

In this program, archival footage, personal recollections, and family photos trace their journey and the indelible mark the Irish have left on "Oilean Ur"—the "fresh land." Visiting several major U.S. cities with large Irish enclaves, the program explores the role played by family, community, and tradition in the Irish immigrants' 100-year transition from day laborers to leaders such as President John F. Kennedy.

"What Does It Mean to Be White? The Invisible Whiteness of Being" (2004, Insight Media, 60 minutes.

In this video, Derald Wing Sue asks whites and nonwhites what it means to be white. The reactions are provocative and reveal how unaware and uncomfortable many white people are with such a question. Sue defines white privilege and explains how it keeps Whites relatively oblivious to the intimidation and oppression felt by nonwhites.

Chapter 6

Southern, Central, and Eastern Europeans

Chapter 6 At-A-Glance

Detailed Outline	Instructor Resources	Print Supplements	Media Supplements	Professor Notes
Sociohistorical Perspective Push-Pull Factors Structural Conditions Societal Reaction	**Lecture Topics:** U.S... white ethnic experience from the late 19th and the 20th century. **Class Activities:** #1	Test Bank **Textbook Review Questions:** #1, 2 & 4	**PowerPoint** **Media:** "Ellis Island: Gateway to America" (1991, Sterling Educational Media, 28 min.) "The Inheritance" (1969, Anti-Defamation League, 45 min.) "Old World, New World" (Films for the Humanities & Sciences, 52 min.) **www.ablongman.com/ parrillo**	
The Slavic Peoples The Poles The Russians The Ukrainians The Hungarians The Gypsies The Italians The Greeks The Portuguese The Armenians	**Lecture Topic:** Push and pull factors associated with each group's immigration, how these strangers adjusted to a new society, cultural diversity in their homeland and the new world.	**Test Bank** **The Ethnic Experience:** Immigrant First Impressions **Textbook Review Questions:** #3	**PowerPoint** **Media:** "American Gypsy: A Stranger in Everybody's Land" (2000, University of California, 79 min.) "The Armenian Americans" (2000, PBS, 57 min.) "The Greek Americans" (1998, PBS, 57 min.) "Lenin and Me" (2004, Insight Media, 52 min.) "The Polish Americans" (1998, PBS, 57 min.) **www.ablongman.com/ parrillo**	
Immigrant Women and Work	**Lecture Topics:** Cultural norms regarding women in the workplace.	Test Bank	**PowerPoint** **www.ablongman.com/ parrillo**	

Southern, Central, and Eastern European Assimilation	**Lecture Topics:** Assimilation, Amalgamation and Accommodation in the new world, who adjusted easiest to the new environment and culture? **Class Activities:** #2	**Test Bank** **The Ethnic Experience:** Education In and Out of the Classroom **The Ethnic Experience:** Bewilderment and Adjustment. **Textbook Review Questions:** #5	**PowerPoint** **Media:** "Euro-American Issues in the U.S.A.." (1992, RMI Media Productions, 60 min.) "European Americans" (2001, Insight Media, 60 min.) "The Italian Gardens of South Brooklyn" (1997, University of California, 26 min.) **www.ablongman.com/ parrillo**	
Sociological Analysis Functionalist View Conflict View Interactionist View	**Lecture Topics:** Compare and contrast the three main theoretical views of immigration and acculturation.	**Test Bank** **Textbook Review Questions:** #6	**PowerPoint** **www.ablongman.com/ parrillo**	

CHAPTER 6

SOUTHERN, CENTRAL, AND EASTERN EUROPEANS

LEARNING OBJECTIVES

1. To examine the white ethnic experience in the late 19th and the 20th century from a sociohistorical perspective

2. To show how minority acceptance can be affected by dominant expectations, structural conditions, and minority adaptation

3. To provide insight into racism as a broader ideology that encompasses whites as well as nonwhites

4. To illustrate the problems engendered in dominant-minority relations by nativist stereotyping and xenophobia

5. To study specifically the Slavic peoples, Poles, Hungarians, Gypsies, Russians, Ukrainians, Italians, Greeks, Portuguese, and Armenians as strangers adjusting to a new society

SUMMARY

1. Millions of European immigrants, the heavy majority of them peasants, journeyed by steamship to America for political and/or economic reasons between 1880 and 1921. Most settled in urban areas and formed their own subcommunities. The men (and often the children) worked at semi-skilled jobs in mines, factories, and on construction crews.

2. Like the immigrants before them, the newcomers came from countries with an agrarian economy. However, they entered an industrialized America where most job opportunities were to be found in the cities. Confined to overcrowded areas in the poorest sections, their adjustment in a new society was not only to a new culture, but also to different working and living conditions.

3. The International Scene boxed feature discusses the anti-immigrant backlash in Italy against Africans and Asians.

4. Nativist reaction included a racist view of these dark-haired, dark-skinned people as undesirables. Jews and Italians were more specific targets because of their greater visibility; nativists indiscriminately grouped all others together.

5. Labor unrest, riots, the Haymarket affair, and strife in Europe—all served to compound the problems of intergroup relations. Finally, Congress responded with restrictive immigration legislation in 1921 and 1924 to reduce substantially the number of immigrants.

6. Many Slavic immigrants became unskilled workers in the coal mines, iron and steel factories, and slaughterhouses in Pennsylvania and the Midwest. Their deprivation and social segregation in ethnic enclaves typify what many groups experienced during this time period. Today, South Slavic peoples still retain their distinct cultural identities.

7. The Polish experience was one of cultural shock, social disorganization, and eventual community stabilization. With an emphasis on preserving of Polish culture and traditions, once including a negative orientation toward education, Polonia today remains somewhat resilient due to new arrivals, with 80 percent of Polish Americans living in the Northeast.

8. Russian immigrants included many ethnic minorities fleeing Czarist Russia. Mostly poor, illiterate peasants, they also had to make the transformation from a rural environment to an industrial one. The Bolshevik Revolution brought others who sought asylum in the United States, but it also fueled a xenophobic reaction against all Russians, epitomized by the infamous Palmer raids. Only 163,000 Russians came to the United States between 1921-1990, a figure surpassed since 1992. Residential clustering by region of origin is common. Most Russian Americans are Orthodox Christians, with wide occupational distribution.

9. Some Ukrainians settled as farmers in the western United States and Canada, but most of the 700,000 who came before 1914 worked in the coal mines and factories of the Northeast and Midwest. About 85,000 Ukrainians came to the United States under the 1948 Displaced Persons Act. Since 1992, over 130,000 new immigrants have arrived.

10. The Hungarians were a religiously diverse people who also created their own ethnic communities and institutions. Most worked in mines and heavy industries, and many became actively involved in the labor unrest of the times. Refugees from World War II and the Hungarian rebellion of 1956 brought tens of thousands more to the United States.

11. Gypsies are an elusive minority and an excellent example of a persistent subculture. Distinguished by their Romany language and their culture, they have patriarchal families and emphasize patri-local residence. Their values and lifestyle encourage illiteracy and distrust of bureaucracies and outside society. *Rom* culture has as its linchpin the concept of *marime,* which sets lines between good and bad, clean and unclean, including the upper and lower halves of the body.

12. Italian immigrants of this period were mostly peasants whose culture was characterized by an emphasis on family and distrust of strangers and education. The extended-family arrangement and cohesive Little Italy communities restricted inter-ethnic friendships, but they insulated the immigrants from the intense societal hostility directed against them. Problems of marginality were especially acute among second-generation Italian-Americans. Upward mobility is more evident among the third generation, but the family ties remain strong. Though lagging behind other European American groups, convergence is beginning and a "twilight of ethnicity" evolving.

13. Greek immigrants settled primarily in ethnic enclaves in the major cities, becoming identified primarily with candy stores and restaurants. Many males came as sojourners and then returned home, but others remained in America. Endogamy, strict child rearing, and emphasis on education were the norms. Economic stability, ethnic pride, and social mobility were typical.

14. Portuguese occupational preferences were mainly fishing and farming and many settled in New England, California, and Hawaii. Assimilation was far more common in Hawaii than in California and New England, possibly because of the plantation economy and population composition there. The greatest number of Portuguese, like other nationalities, came in the late nineteenth and early twentieth centuries to work in the factories. Over 65,000 have migrated here since 1980.

15. Armenians, a persecuted minority like the Jews, are similar to them in their emphasis on education, family life, and social mobility. Their unique language and alphabet, together with their religion, make them a very cohesive ethnic group.

16. Typically, married women did not work outside the home, although working at home (laundry, sewing, crafts) or taking in boarders were ways to augment family income. Mostly, single women aged 16 to 24 were in the labor force, about one-third each blue-collar workers, domestics, or among native-born women, in white-collar positions.

17. Given the diversity among this group of immigrants, no general assessment of their assimilation is possible. Agrarian backgrounds, religious differences, illiteracy and low educational values slowed the process for many, but some—Armenians, Greek, Jews—were able to mainstream more quickly, given their greater emphasis on education.

18. Functionalists examine the millions of new immigrants as a needed labor pool for America's rapid industrialization and as fervent patriotic converts. Accompanying slums, crime, and labor strife were dysfunctions caused by rapid social change, in time corrected.

19. Conflict analysis examines how American industrialists exploited immigrant workers. Only through aroused class-consciousness and the labor union movement did the workers, with much risk and sacrifice, gain their share of the American Dream.

20.   Interactionists emphasize the social interpretations of the native-born population, who saw physically and culturally distinct people settling in massive numbers in crowded, high-crime slums and then assumed the social problems and labor unrest were caused by the newcomers.

CLASS ACTIVITIES

1.   A guest speaker from an ethnic organization could tell the class about the history and purpose of that organization in promoting their cultural heritage.

2.   Discuss the settlement of these Europeans in your area. Do current statistics of the local population reflect migration of European descendants or geographic longevity? What factors do students think contribute to this pattern?

INTERNET RESOURCES

At this book's Web site (http://www.ablongman.com/parrillo), students should select the cover icon, then Chapter 6 to find a variety of links, exercises, and activities pertinent to this content.

MEDIA MATERIALS

"American Gypsy: A Stranger in Everybody's Land" (2000, University of California, 79 min.)

America is home to one million Gypsies, or Rom, whose rich culture has long been mysterious to outsiders. Shot over the course of five years, this extraordinary documentary is the first ever allowed to break the wall of secrecy that protects the universally persecuted Romany people and their culture.

"The Armenian Americans" (2000, PBS, 57 minutes)

Bonded by a distinct alphabet, language, foods and the church that is the worldwide repository of their cultural identity, Armenian Americans preserve their cultural consciousness with an unspoken passing of responsibility that resonates in personal recollections from three generations of Armenian Americans.

"Ellis Island: Gateway to America" (1991, Sterling Educational Media, 28 minutes)

Vincent Parrillo narrates this award-winning PBS documentary blending historic photos and film footage with a present-day tour through the main building. With anecdotes and poignant commentary, this inspiring program delineates the significance of Ellis Island to all Americans, regardless of background.

"Euro-American Issues in the U.S.A." (1992, RMI Media Productions, 60 minutes)

Examines the diversity among the many European ethnic groups in the United States, and their problems relating to merging into the majority Anglo culture and yet retaining individual language and customs.

"European Americans" (2001, Insight Media, 60 minutes)

In this video, students examine the impact of European-American culture both nationally and globally. The program considers the role and significance of European languages and religions in the United States and around the world. It features examples from the history and experiences of Polish and Italian Americans.

"The Greek Americans" (1998, PBS, 57 minutes)

Tells of Greek immigrants organizing communities in many U.S. cities to keep alive their native language, culture and religion. Closely bound by tradition, Greeks changed the U.S. physical landscape with the rounded domes and distinctive crosses of the Greek Orthodox Church and the cultural landscape with accomplishments in the arts, politics and education.

"The Inheritance" (1969, Anti-Defamation League, 45 minutes)

Historic film footage and dramatic still photographs document the America of the late 19th and early 20th centuries and the economic, social, and cultural impact of the great waves of immigrants. Parallels white ethnic involvement in labor union movement with the civil rights movement.

"The Italian Gardens of South Brooklyn" (1997, University of California, 26 minutes)

This infectiously enjoyable and constantly inventive documentary illustrates how "a mixture of old-world values and new-world horse sense" invigorates the traditional Italian-American community of South Brooklyn and infuses it with a strong respect for family, friends, and neighborhood.

"Lenin and Me" (2004, Insight Media, 52 minutes)

In this documentary, Arthur Chidlovski, a Russian-born immigrant living in the U.S., locates the meaning of his own past within the momentous history of his former country. The film shows how one individual's subjective viewpoint can be a portal into an entire nation's political, cultural, and economic history. It portrays the confusion and the betrayal that many former Soviets faced when trying to understand "Uncle" Lenin: a brilliant political leader and yet ruthless and cruel dictator.

"Old World, New World" (Films for the Humanities & Sciences, 52 minutes)

The story of 35 million Europeans who left their troubled homelands for the promise of freedom and opportunity, and the hardships of the transatlantic voyage they endured to reach America.

"The Polish Americans" (1998, PBS, 57 minutes)

Using vintage film footage, family photos, personal recollections and experiences, this documentary takes viewers to the little Polska (Poland) across the United States, from New York City and Schenectady to Cleveland and Chicago, where parents instill in their children the virtues and values of their native land and a love of its traditions.

Chapter 7

The Native Americans

Chapter 7 At-A-Glance

Detailed Outline	Instructor Resources	Print Supplements	Media Supplements	Professor Notes
Sociohistorical Perspective Early Encounters Cultural Strains Differing Values	**Lecture Topics:** Initial Native American experience with the white man.	**Test Bank Textbook Review Questions: #1**	**PowerPoint Media:** "As Long as the Grass Shall Grow" (2001 Ambrose Video, 60 min.) "In the White Man's Image" (1991, video, PBS Video, 60 min.) **www.ablongman.com/ parrillo**	
Values and Social Structure	**Lecture Topic:** Native Americans' close relationship with nature. Childrearing practices. Gender roles. **Class Activities: #1**	**Test Bank**	**PowerPoint Media:** "The Right to Their Own Lands" (1993, Films for the Humanities and Sciences, 28 min.) "Native-American Traditions" (1994, video, Insight Media, 60 min.) **www.ablongman.com/ parrillo**	
Stereotyping of Native Americans	**Lecture Topics:** Negative representation of Native Americans	**Test Bank Textbook Review Questions: #2**	**PowerPoint www.ablongman.com/ parrillo**	

Changes in Government Policy Indian Removal Act Reservations and Dependence Indian Reorganization Act The Relocation Program The Termination Act	**Lecture Topics:** Government Actions Toward Native Americans	**Test Bank**	**PowerPoint Media:** "Little Big Horn: The Native American View" (2003, Insight Media, 25 min.) "Teaching Indians to be White" (1992, Films for the Humanities & Sciences, 28 min.) **www.ablongman.com/ parrillo**	
Present-Day Native American Life Population Employment Life Expectancy Alcohol Abuse Education Housing **Natural Resources** Exploitation and Emerging Control "Dances with Garbage and Nuclear Waste" Water Rights	**Lecture Topics:** Life experiences and living conditions of Native Americans in the 21st century. **Class Activities:** #2 & 3	**Test Bank The International Scene:** A New Treaty Ends Exploitation. **The Ethnic Experience:** Boarding School Experience. **Textbook Review Questions:** #5	**Power Point Media:** "Gambling: Does It Benefit Society?" (1997, Films for the Humanities & Sciences, 29 min.) "Native American Cultures in the U.S.A..: Part One and Part Two" (1992, RMI Media Productions, 60 min.) "On and Off the Reservation a Native American" (1997, Insight Media, 18 min.) **www.ablongman.com/ parrillo**	
Red Power Pan-Indianism Alcatraz Wounded Knee **The Courts Bureau of Indian Affairs Native American Assimilation**	**Lecture Topics:** Native American organizations, protests, and rights.	**Test Bank The Ethnic Experience:** A Formal Apology to the Indian People **Textbook Review Questions:** #4	**PowerPoint Media:** In Whose Honor?" (1996, New Day Films, 46 min.) "More Than Bows and Arrows" (1992, Insight Media, 60 min.) "Rebellion" (1992, Films for the Humanities and Sciences, 24 min.) **www.ablongman.com/ parrillo**	
Sociological Analysis Functionalist View Conflict View Interactionist View	**Lecture Topics:** Compare and contrast the three main theoretical views of immigration and acculturation.	**Test Bank**	**PowerPoint www.ablongman.com/ parrillo**	

CHAPTER 7

THE NATIVE AMERICANS

LEARNING OBJECTIVES

1.   To study the Native-American experience from a sociohistorical perspective

2.   To acquaint students with Native-American values, social structure, and present-day life

3.   To examine the wide range of dominant and minority response patterns found throughout Indian-White relations

4.   To familiarize students with the diversity among Native-Americans, whether they live on reservations or in urban areas

5.   To study Native-American militancy today, the role of the Bureau of Indian Affairs (BIA), and exploitation of reservation Native Americans to meet energy demands

SUMMARY

1.   Misunderstandings, false stereotypes, and racism have plagued Indian-White relations for 500 years, during which time many different patterns in majority-minority relations occurred.

2.   Europeans first manifested a benign ethnocentrism in their early contacts with the Indians, which often degenerated into enslavement, exploitation, or annihilation. Differences in economic development and dominant attitudes in the United States and Latin America resulted in the Indians' achievement of different social, economic, and political statuses.

3.   Initial cooperation between Indians and Whites along the eastern seaboard of the United States gradually lessened as the settlements became more stabilized. Increased interaction and cultural diffusion resulted in the Indians becoming less self-sufficient and economically dependent on the whites.

4. Native American values differed markedly from those of most White Americans in their values and practices regarding nature, land use, childrearing, and social control. Each member of the tribe had gender-specific role responsibilities, which created a cooperative, but not egalitarian, arrangement. Native Americans have a holistic or symbiotic view of nature, seeing all existence as interrelated. Whites tend to separate and categorize elements of experience achieving spectacular advances in science and technology, but at the cost of a fragmented approach to life.

5. Some of the more common but false stereotypes of Native Americans have been those of bloodthirsty savages, silent or aloof people, and the simplistic Hollywood picture of Indians who are either noble or vicious.

6. The Cherokee offer a tragic case study of one tribe's successful efforts at assimilation being rejected by the dominant group. After eight years of legal maneuvers, the federal government expelled the Cherokee from their land and resettled them in Oklahoma. More than four thousand died during the forced march to that destination.

7. Official government policy shifted in the mid-nineteenth century from annihilation and expulsion to segregation and isolation. The after effects of that policy are still evident today. Attempts to change Indian culture and lifestyles worsened their situation, deprived them of even more land, and created a subclass of people completely dependent on the federal bureaucracy for most aspects of their lives.

8. The 1930s witnessed an improvement in the federal government's treatment of the Indians, but by the 1950s efforts at assimilation again resulted in a worsening of the Indians' situation. Relocation-resettlement in urban areas was a failure, and termination—ending federal responsibility to selected Indian tribes—resulted in disorganization and financial ruin to some, such as the Menominee.

9. The Native American birth rate is almost twice the national average, partly reflected in their increase from 2.1 to 2.5 million between 1990 and 2000. Large-scale chronic unemployment on the reservations is a serious problem. Deaths from vehicular accidents, liver disease, diabetes, homicide and suicide are all well above the national average.

10. Blistering Senate attacks on the BIA, its educational policy, and boarding schools has resulted in some changes, notably in local control of schools, but numerous problems remain. Substandard housing remains a problem, with many homes without indoor plumbing and electricity.

11. Energy demands have continued the exploitation of the Native American, often with BIA complicity, up to the present day. The Blackfeet of Montana faced strip-mining efforts of their sacred Sweet Grass Hills until organized efforts halted unrestricted access. About 12,000 Navajo were evicted from Big Mountain in 1980-1998 as part of a coal strip-mining agreement with the Hopi in the same region. Organized protests and violence

against the Lake Superior Chippewa challenged their fishing rights under treaty protection. The Council of Energy Resource Tribes (CERT) had some success with preventing exploitation of mineral resources, but toxic dumping on, or poisoning of, reservation lands (Rosebud Sioux, Mescalero Apache, St. Regis Mohawk) is a new reality. Water use disputes, particularly in the Southwest still threaten the economic independence of many tribes.

12.   In the 1960s, partly inspired by the civil rights movement, Native Americans became more militant in their demands and actions. Pan-Indianism, an attempt to establish racial-group identity instead of tribal identities, did not find complete acceptance. Some gains have occurred, such as the return of 48,000 acres to the Taos Pueblo in New Mexico and recent court decisions on fishing rights and illegal transfer of Native American land.

13.   Further complicating Native American life is the fact that a remote, complex bureaucracy dominates every aspect of that life. Expert groups have recommended massive restructuring of the BIA, but no significant changes have occurred thus far.

14.   Nearly 70 percent of the 2.5 million Native Americans live in urban areas. They are more likely to be working than those living on reservations, but usually require about five years of urban residence to see improved income earnings. Although they do not reside in ethnic enclaves, their other behavior patterns parallel other urban minority groups. Assimilation is quite low and problems of adaptation intensify such problems as drunkenness and alcoholism. A 1994 study revealed higher infant mortality, tuberculosis, injury and alcohol-related death rates among urban Native Americans than those living in rural areas.

15.   Native Americans arguably have had the greatest impact on U.S. culture in geographic names, vocabulary, and material artifacts.

16.   Despite forced assimilation efforts over generations, Native Americans remain a persistent subculture attempting to preserve their cultural identity, values, and practices.

17.   Many people continue to find the paternalistic treatment of Native Americans functional and resist needed adjustments to restore their self-sufficiency. Illustrative of conflict theory, past and present exploitation undermines Native American life, but organized efforts have caused some social change. Social interpretations of both racial groups toward one another from past to present prompt misunderstanding and conflict.

18.   The International Scene boxed feature discusses a recent treaty between Canada and the Nisga'a. The first Ethnic Experiences box gives a firsthand account of a boarding school experience, and the next gives an excerpt of a formal BIA apology to Native Americans.

CLASS ACTIVITIES

1.   A Native American guest speaker could tell your class about tribal values, beliefs, and customs, as well as reasons for preserving that heritage.

2.   If you are located near a reservation, have a tribal spokesperson speak to your class about reservation conditions.

3.   Encourage students to write to BIA for literature and then compare that material to other government data on Native American health, income, etc.

INTERNET RESOURCES

At this book's Web site (http://www.ablongman.com/parrillo), students should select the cover icon, then Chapter 7 to find a variety of links, exercises, and activities pertinent to this content.

MEDIA MATERIALS

"As Long as the Grass Shall Grow" (2001, Ambrose Video, 60 minutes)

This film depicts the once great hunting grounds of the Lakota, once misnamed "Sioux." as desolate lands alongside wealthy white towns and tourist attractions.   For the Lakota, there is little left of the great hunting grounds but ghettos, malnutrition, alcoholism, soaring teenage suicide, and the acquiescence to white authority and its system of justice.

"Gambling: Does It Benefit Society?" (1997, Films for the Humanities & Sciences, 29 minutes)

Some states and Native American tribes rely on legalized gambling as an essential source of income. But has this income really benefited those it was supposed to help? Are casinos investing in communities, as suggested by supporters, or diverting the money elsewhere? Compares living conditions in communities with casinos with other similar communities.

"In the White Man's Image" (1991, PBS Video, 60 minutes)

In the 1870s, the motto at the Carlisle School for Indians was "kill the Indian and save the man." This program investigates the tragic long-term consequences of a humanist experiment gone terribly wrong.

"In Whose Honor?" (1996, New Day Films, 46 minutes)

>   Takes a critical look at the long-running practice of "honoring" American Indians as mascots and nicknames in sports. Also discusses issues of racism, stereotypes, minority representation and the powerful effects of mass-media imagery.

"The Indian Experience in the 20th Century" (1992, Films for the Humanities & Sciences, 28 minutes)

>   Depicts the militancy of Mohawk protesting the use of the sacred lands as a golf course, the Cree fighting the construction of a hydroelectric dam, and the murder and suppression of indigenous people in Latin America. Also profiles the success story of the Kuna in Panama.

"Little Big Horn: The Native American View" (2003, Insight Media, 25 minutes)

>   This program examines what really happened during Custer's last stand, the U.S. cavalry's decisive defeat at the hands of Sioux and Cheyenne warriors in 1876. It relates the Native-American side of the story, and includes profiles of Custer, Sitting Bull, Crazy Horse, and Gall.

"More Than Bows and Arrows" (1992, Insight Media, 60 minutes)

>   Shows the impact of Native Americans on the political, social, and cultural development on U.S. government, agriculture, transportation, architecture, science, technology, the arts, medicine, and language. Narrated by M. Scott Momaday.

"Native American Cultures in the U.S.A.: Part One" (1992, RMI Media Productions, 60 minutes)

>   Presents information about early populations of Native Americans; the rights of Native Americans; stereotypes; treaty disputes; the Colville land allotments.

"Native American Cultures in the U.S.A.: Part Two" (1992, RMI Media Productions, 60 minutes)

>   Case study of the controversy regarding displaying remains of ancient Native Americans at Dickson Mounds Museum Burial Grounds, Lewiston, Illinois. Also covers Native Americans and respect for the environment.

"Native-American Traditions" (1994, Insight Media, 60 minutes)

This video examines Native-American religion and culture, showing the connection between Native-American spirituality and New Age religions. Discusses the differences between Native-American and other religions, and ecological and feminist issues.

"On and Off the Reservation a Native American" (1997, Insight Media, 18 minutes)

Portrays contemporary Native Americans striving to protect their culture and heritage while succeeding in mainstream America. Examines the roles of education, family, and tribal affiliation; traditional practices; and economic issues that complicate reservation life.

"Rebellion" (1992, Films for the Humanities & Sciences, 24 minutes)

"Why do they think we have no feelings?" asks a girl. "Because we are Indians?" War against the native inhabitants has been going on uninterrupted since 1492—because one side considers the land sacred and the other wants to own it. Shows footage of the Ona of Tierra del Fuego; filmed in 1913, the tribe is now extinct, replaced by grazing sheep. It also shows what happened at Wounded Knee and why and the result, down to our own day.

"The Right to Their Own Lands" (1993, Films for the Humanities & Sciences, 28 minutes)

Depicts contrasting values about land ownership among Native Americans and whites. Living either on wasteland reservations in regions rich in resources, or in areas steadily shrinking as roads are built, rivers channeled and forests destroyed, the native peoples also cannot stomach the condescension of the white man, with his certainty that he knows what is best for the native. "They can keep their knowledge. We just want to be left alone."

"Teaching Indians to be White" (1992, Films for the Humanities & Sciences, 28 minutes)

Shows the culture clash Native American children encounter in the schools, whether they are religious, residential, or public. Shows the Florida Seminole resisting integration, the Miccosukee accepting integration, and the Cree taking back their own schools.

Chapter 8
East and Southeast Asian Americans

Chapter 8 At-A-Glance

Detailed Outline	Instructor Resources	Print Supplements	Media Supplements	Professor Notes
Sociohistorical Perspective	**Lecture Topics:** Push and pull factors for East and Southeast Asians' immigration to the U.S.	**Test Bank Textbook Review Questions:** #1 & 3	**PowerPoint Media:** "Asian Americans: (1993, Insight Media, 3 volumes, 30 min. each) "A Nation of Immigrants: The Chinese-American Experience" (1991, Films for the Humanities and Sciences, 20 min.) **www.ablongman.com/parrillo**	
Cultural Attributes	**Lecture Topic:** traditional and conservative family values. Strict control of emotional expression. **Class Activities:** #1 & 2	**Test Bank Textbook Review Question:** #5	**PowerPoint Media:** "Asian-American Cultures" (1992, Insight Media, 60 min.) "Asian-American Cultures in the U.S.A." (1992, RMI Media Productions, 60 min.) "The Chinese Americans" (2002, PBS, 57 min.) **www.ablongman.com/parrillo**	

Asian Immigrants The Chinese The Japanese The Filipinos The Koreans The Vietnamese The Cambodians The Laotions The Thai	**Lecture Topics:** Structural conditions upon arrival of each new immigrant group. Recent immigration patterns. **International Scene:** The Difference Between Race and Culture. **The Ethnic Experience:** The First Korean Women in the United States. The Desperate Bid for Freedom.	**Test Bank Textbook Review Questions: #4**	**PowerPoint Media:** "Being Hmong Means Being Free" (2000, NAATA, 56 min.) "Filipino Americans: Discovering their Past for the Future" (1994, NAATA, 54 min.) "First Person Plural" (2002, NAATA, 56 min.) "From a Different Shore: The Japanese-American Experience" (1994, Films for the Humanities and Sciences, 50 min.) **www.ablongman.com/parrillo**	
Ethnoviolence	**Lecture Topics:** Majority group reaction. **Class Activity: #4**	**Test Bank Textbook Review Questions: #2 & 6**	**Power Point Media:** "Korean Americans" (Films for the Humanities and Sciences, 50 min.) **www.ablongman.com/parrillo**	
The Model-Minority Stereotype	**Lecture Topics:** East and Southeast Asian Assimilation **The Ethnic Experience:** The Struggle to Adapt. **Class Activity: #3**	**Test Bank Textbook Review Question: #7**	**PowerPoint Media:** "The Asianization of America" (Films for the Humanities and Sciences, 26 min.) "Between Worlds" (1998, University of California, 57 min.) "Vietnamese Americans: The New Generation" (2001, University of California, 33 min.) **www.ablongman.com/parrillo**	

Sociological Analysis Functionalist View Conflict View Interactionist View	Lecture Topics: Compare and contrast the three main theoretical views of immigration and acculturation.	Test Bank Textbook Review Question: #8	PowerPoint www.ablongman.com/parrillo	

CHAPTER 8

EAST AND SOUTHEAST ASIAN AMERICANS

LEARNING OBJECTIVES

1. To study the experiences of the Chinese, Japanese, Filipinos, Koreans, Vietnamese, Laotians, and other Asians from a sociohistorical perspective

2. To show how racism, whether obscured in labor, social, or national security concerns, created conflict situations for many Asian Americans

3. To examine and contrast past and present patterns of interaction and adjustment by Asian immigrants

4. To discuss more recent immigrants, such as the Koreans and Vietnamese, and the similarities and dissimilarities of their experiences as compared with those of earlier Asian immigrants.

SUMMARY

1. Racist hostility, an imbalance in the Asian sexual ratio, and economic competition were important factors in the problems Asian immigrants encountered on the West Coast.

2. A negative stereotype preceded the first Chinese arrival in California in the 1850s. Coming as sojourners, they worked in railroad gangs, manufacturing, and other endeavors. By the mid-1870s, racial prejudice grew into sinophobia, culminating in the Chinese Exclusion Act of 1882. Anti-Chinese riots, expulsion, and job and housing discrimination were frequent. The Chinatowns, situated in low-rent ghetto areas, became home to many, where benevolent and protective organizations offered assistance. Internal factionalism limited the Chinese community's insulation against hostility. Today Chinatowns are larger and more crowded than they were eighty years ago. Although tourist attractions, they are slum communities with growing problems of delinquency among more recent arrivals. The Chinese American population has tripled since 1980 to 2.4 million in 2000, with a bipolar occupational distribution in professional/ technical and in low-skilled service occupations.

3. The Japanese began emigrating in larger numbers at the turn of the century, settling on the West Coast where anti-Asian feelings remained intense. Coming in families and intending to stay, they encountered labor union hostility and discriminatory legislation. The incarceration of 110,000 Japanese-Americans in World War II, 63 percent of them American-born, was a racist action unjustified by national security reasons. This act of expulsion and imprisonment weakened Japanese subcommunities and institutions, which

enhanced assimilation. Since World War II, Japanese have had more schooling than all other groups, more outgroup dating and marriage, and increased upward mobility. Half of all Japanese Americans are native-born Americans. Japanese Americans have a high degree of structural assimilation, especially evident in outgroup dating and exogamy. In recent years Japanese sojourners, the Kai-sha, have come to work for a few years in United States branch offices of their homeland companies.

4. The International Scene box profiles Japan's unexpected experience with culturally distinct Brazilian Japanese.

5. With the Philippines a U.S. possession, tens of thousands of Filipino males came to the mainland in the twentieth century to fill the void created by various restrictive legislative acts against other foreigners, including Mexicans. Labor union antagonism during the Depression years and the scarcity of Filipino women, which resulted in the men seeking female companionship outside their ethnic group, increased Caucasian-Filipino tensions. The Philippines were granted independence in 1935 and this meant virtually no further Filipino immigration until 1965, when the quota system was abolished. Since then, Filipino Americans have almost doubled each decade to number over 1.4 million in 1990, thus constituting the second largest Asian American group in the United States.

6. Early Korean immigrants journeyed mostly to Hawaii to work on sugar plantations, although a few thousand did continue on to California. The Korean War brought many refugees and war brides to the United States, but most of the 1.1 million Korean Americans today have come since 1970, often working in professional, technical, or managerial fields, or as a middleman minority in small business enterprises such as green grocers. Their self-employment rate of 11.9 percent far exceeds all other minority groups. Deeply entrenched in the Korean immigrant ethos, self-employment normally becomes a reality with aid from the *kye,* a rotating-credit association not unlike others found among the Chinese and Japanese. Although faring well economically, most Koreans rank low in social distance studies, indicating structural assimilation to be virtually nonexistent at this time.

6. Most Vietnamese in the United States are refugees from that war-ravaged country. Resettled in all fifty states, but more numerous in California, Texas, and Pennsylvania, they formed their own self-help organizations. They encountered some resistance and discrimination, but since many possessed a middle class background and job skills, adjustment has been relatively easy. The acculturation process has already lessened their traditional extended-family arrangement, but other traditional values and beliefs remain strong. More recent arrivals have been less skilled and educated, and their acculturation problems more pronounced.

7. Laotians number about 169,000, the greatest concentration being the Hmong. Coming from a pre-literate society, they are slowly acculturating, after several years on welfare relief. Cultural dissonance between foreign-born parents and Americanized adolescents typically affects the Hmong family.

8. In 1999, violent incidents against Asian Pacific Americans increased 57 percent over 1998. The frequency of anti-Asian violent incidents suggests a pattern, not local isolated incidents. The conflict between black neighborhood residents and Korean storeowners that had occurred in several cities was perhaps epitomized in the May 1992 Los Angeles riot when about 2,300 Korean-owned stores were damaged or destroyed.

9. The educational and financial success of many Asian Americans gave rise to a model minority stereotype succeeding with a color-free, problem-free, interventionist-free integration into U.S. society. Such a portrait not only places enormous pressure on Asian American youth to succeed, but also ignores the poverty, welfare, crime, exploitation, sickness, and despair encountered by other Asian newcomers.

10. As with all groups, rates of assimilation vary greatly among and within Asian/Pacific groups. As a whole though, they have the highest median family income of all groups, and the second lowest poverty rate (after whites). A greater proportion become U.S. citizens than any other foreign-born group, and they live in less segregated areas than other minority groups. By 2000, about half of all native-born Asian Americans had a non-Asian spouse, revealing increased blending with other U.S. groups.

11. From a functionalist viewpoint, Asian immigrants provide a needed labor pool in agriculture, low-skill jobs, technical and professional fields. Economic exploitation, both past and present, dominate the conflict analysis of their immigrant experience. In the past, Asians were an enigma to others on the West Coast; today, the difficult problems of social interaction weigh most heavily on the Indochinese refugees facing a bewildering urban society.

CLASS ACTIVITIES

1. An Asian American guest speaker, perhaps from your own faculty, could tell the class about shared cultural hallmarks among most Asians as well as the differences among them.

2. An instructor of philosophy or sociology of religion could inform the class about Eastern religions and their social control mechanisms.

3. An educator from a local public school system could inform the class about its bilingual programs for Asian students and changing student population.

4. Divide your class into small groups to exchange knowledge about recent instances of prejudice, discrimination or ethnoviolence against Asians, then report to entire class.

INTERNET RESOURCES

At this book's Web site (http://www.ablongman.com/parrillo), students should select the cover icon, then Chapter 8 to find a variety of links, exercises, and activities pertinent to this content.

MEDIA MATERIALS

"After Silence: Civil Rights and the Japanese-American Experience" (2003, Insight Media, 30 minutes)

What does it mean to be an American in a time of uncertainty and fear? This program examines the fragile nature of civil rights and explores WWII Japanese-American internment through the lens of September 11. It looks at the story of Frank Kitamoto, who spent more than three years in an internment camp, as he stresses the need to safeguard individuals' constitutional rights – especially in times of crisis.

"Amerasians" (1999, Insight Media, 52 minutes)

The Vietnam War left behind bomb craters, napalmed forests, vast casualties, and about 100,000 fatherless children. In 1988, the Amerasian Homecoming Act offered Vietnamese with an American parent a ticket to the United States and a six-month allowance. More than 38,000 people have taken the offer. This video profiles Amerasians who have moved to the United States or who are about to leave Vietnam. It considers the shock of moving to a new country and discusses the complexity of multicultural identity.

"An Asian-American Story: Life Review Interview With Derald Wing Sue" (2004, Insight Media, 60 minutes)

"Derald Wing Sue is an authority on multicultural counseling and therapy. This video discusses his origins in Oregon and how school experiences with discrimination led him to multicultural awareness and pride.

"Asian-American Cultures" (1992, Insight Media, 60 minutes)

Describes the ethnic groups making up the Asian-American community, their similarities, differences, and intergenerational problems. It also considers why some groups have achieved greater economic success, leading to their being called the "model minority."

"Asian-American Cultures in the U.S.A." (1992, RMI Media Productions, 60 minutes)

Overview of the many groups classified as Asian Americans, and discussion of their similarities and differences. Also includes contrasting attitudes between first- and second-generation Asian Americans.

"Asian Americans" (1993, Insight Media, 3 volumes, 30 minutes each)

Examines cultural heritage and unique traditions of Chinese, Japanese and Korean Americans. Discusses when and why each group immigrated to the United States and probes how cultural identity differs among generations.

"The Asianization of America" (Films for the Humanities & Sciences, 26 minutes)

Examines the role of Asian Americans half a century after the repeal of the Chinese Exclusion Act, seeking to determine what accounts for Asians' startling successes in academia and to what extent they can, should, or want to blend into the U.S. melting pot.

"Becoming American: The Chinese Experience" (2003, Insight Media, 3 segments, 90 minutes each)

Through interviews with historians, descendants of Chinese immigrants, and recent Chinese immigrants, this program explores what it means to become an American of Chinese origin or descent. It examines the impact of the 1882 Chinese Exclusion Act and discusses how the new immigration laws of 1965 were a turning point for the Chinese in America.

"Being Hmong Means Being Free" (2000, NAATA, 56 minutes)

Focusing on a Hmong immigrant community in Wisconsin, this documentary offers a comprehensive look at many fundamental concepts and practices of the ancient Hmong culture and relates the difficulties that have arisen from trying to follow those traditions in a new country where the language barrier, limited employment opportunities, and xenophobia present everyday challenges. This documentary also explores how dramatically life has changed for the Hmong in the space of a generation.

"Between Worlds" (1998, University of California, 57 minutes)

This deeply moving portrait of the struggles of recent Vietnamese immigrants to create new lives for themselves is an excellent depiction of the difficult process of becoming American. It is an incisive historical document and a profound emotional experience.

"The Chinese Americans" (2002, PBS, 57 minutes)

Examines the roles Chinese schools, family and district associations, and religious organizations—whether Buddhist, Taoist, Confuscist or Christian—played in transforming Chinese immigrants into Chinese Americans while maintaining the traditions of the culture. The program explores this yin and yang of the old and the new, a balance between the archetypes so eagerly embraced by mainstream America and the desire to assimilate.

"Filipino Americans: Discovering their Past for the Future" (1994, NAATA, 54 minutes)

Award-winning producer John Wehman offers an in-depth history of Filipino Americans through interviews with historians, archival photos and documents, providing a 400-year chronicle of one of the largest ethnic groups in the United States is explored.

"First Person Plural" (2000, NAATA, 56 minutes)

Explores not only the particular nuances of international and trans-racial adoption but the broader cultural landscape of U.S. society over the past several decades. This story of an adopted Korean child is about how we define family, how we define self, the importance of our ties to individual and collective histories, and the reconciling of different identities and moral contradictions. This film challenges the notion of cultural assimilation and begs for alternative ways of looking at culture, race, family and identity.

"From a Different Shore: The Japanese-American Experience" (1994, Films for the Humanities & Sciences, 50 minutes)

Explores the Japanese-American experience, starting with the first immigrants from Japan, the *Issel,* through to the experiences of their grandchildren, told through the lives of three families. They offer their view of the United States and what it means and has meant to be an American of Japanese ancestry.

"Korean Americans" (Films for the Humanities & Sciences, 50 minutes)

Profiles first-generation Korean Americans seeking to retain their traditional cultural values while adjusting to life in the U.S. They come into frequent and violent conflict with inner city African Americans, and seek, through their own ethnic civic organizations, to overcome the rejection of the community around them.

"A Nation of Immigrants: The Chinese-American Experience" (1991, Films for the Humanities & Sciences, 20 minutes)

Explores the plight of Chinese immigrants, attracted to the U.S. by the Gold Rush and the need for farm and railroad laborers, only to experience extremely hard work, pitifully low wages, racial discrimination, riots and discriminatory laws.

"Vietnamese Americans: The New Generation" (2001, University of California, 33 minutes)

Through candid interviews with first- and second-generation Vietnamese Americans, this program documents the process of assimilation into American culture of refugees from the former Republic of Vietnam. Topics includes stresses on the family unit caused by cultural and generational differences, gang membership and drug abuse among the young, anti-Vietnamese racial bias, and feelings about relations between the U.S. and Vietnam.

Chapter 9

Other Asian and Middle Eastern Americans

Chapter 9 At-A-Glance

Detailed Outline	Instructor Resources	Print Supplements	Media Supplements	Professor Notes
Sociohistorical Perspective	**Lecture Topics:** Push and pull factors for Asian and Middle Eastern immigrants coming to the U.S.	Test Bank	**PowerPoint Media:** "Beyond the Veil: Are Iranian Women Rebelling?" (1997, Films for the Humanities & Sciences, 22 min.) **www.ablongman.com /parrillo**	
The Asian and Middle Eastern Immigrants The Asian Indians The Syrian/Lebanese The Palestinians The Iranians The Iraqis The Turks The Pakistanis	**Lecture Topics:** Structural Conditions. Majority and minority response. Recent immigration trends. **Class Activities:** #3	**Test Bank The Ethnic Experience:** Values, Identity, and Acceptance **The Ethnic Experience:** First Encounters with the U.S. Ethnicity and Language **Textbook Review Questions:** #2 & 4	**PowerPoint Media:** "Arab Americans" (2001, Insight Media, 60 min.) "The Arabs: Who They Are, and Who They Are Not" (1991, Films for the Humanities & Sciences, 30 min.) "Conquering America" (1990, Films for the Humanities & Sciences, 30 min.) "Palestinian Portraits" (1987, First Run/Icarus Films, 22 min.) **www.ablongman.com /parrillo**	

Asian and Middle Easterners' Assimilation	**Lecture Topics:** Adjustments and adaptations made to become Americans. **Class Activities: #1 & 2**	**Test Bank Textbook Review Questions: #1 & 3**	**Power Point Media:** "Beneath Chicago: Growing Up Arab and Female in Chicago" (1996, Arab Film, 30 min.) "In My Own Skin: The Complexity of Living as Arab in America" (2001, Insight Media, 15 min.) "Tales From Arab Detroit" (1994, New Day Films, 45 min.) **www.ablongman.com /parrillo**	
Sociological Analysis Functionalist View Conflict View Interactionist View	**Lecture Topics:** Compare and contrast the three main theoretical views of immigration and acculturation.	**Test Bank Textbook Review Questions: #5**	**PowerPoint www.ablongman.com /parrillo**	

CHAPTER 9

OTHER ASIAN AND MIDDLE EASTERN AMERICANS

LEARNING OBJECTIVES

1. To examine, from a sociohistorical perspective those immigrant groups coming from the regions situated between Western and Eastern thought and philosophy

2. To acquaint students with minority groups who are often ignored but are nevertheless an important part of the minority experience in America

3. To study immigrant groups from the Developing World, whose numbers have dramatically increased since the immigration regulation changes in 1965

4. To examine new patterns of adjustment emerging among today's middle-class Other Asian and Middle Eastern Americans

SUMMARY

1. Overpopulation and poverty in their homelands, combined with America's promise of a better chance in life, account for the migration of many non-Western immigrants. For others, educational or career opportunities are the magnet. Current immigration regulations, rapid air travel, and improved communications encourage the migration.

2. Many of these immigrants are trained professionals or skilled technicians who enter job positions with middle-class status. Because either they have a sojourner orientation or they are simply under no pressure to conform in order to succeed, they can enjoy the available opportunities and still retain their cultural ties. Also among them are tens of thousands of students, workers, and business people staying in the United States for a limited period.

3. Asian Indian immigration consisted initially of agricultural laborers migrating to the West Coast in the early twentieth century. Their experiences were similar to those of other Asians: they encountered hostility, discriminatory laws, and discrimination in housing and employment. Many returned home between 1920 and 1940. Those who remained in small rural communities became only slightly acculturated. Asian Indian immigration now exceeds in one year what the total immigration was from 1901 to 1965. Many today are skilled professionals or trained technicians leaving an overpopulated homeland where severe deprivation is common. They experience both guilt feelings about leaving and problems with raising their children according to their traditions.

4.   The International Scene box describes the Asian Indian experience in South Africa, making for a comparative analysis to the U.S. experience.

5.   Over one million Arab Americans now live in the United States. Many are a sophisticated, cosmopolitan people seeking to preserve their heritage. About 91 percent of all Arab Americans live in urban areas, some in recognizable ethnic neighborhoods, but others in more dispersed settlement patterns. Despite their desire for peaceful integration into American society, Arab Americans sometimes fall victim to media stereotypes and misled identification with Middle East extremists.

6.   The Syrian-Lebanese were bonded together by their Jewish, Christian, or Moslem faiths, not by political authority or regional residence. They settled mostly in cities, often displacing the Irish in standard invasion-succession patterns. Family structure was an important factor in their stability and upward mobility, often occurred in the first generation. Evidence of assimilation, including large-scale intermarriage, exists.

7.   Palestinian Americans often feel unfairly stereotyped and isolated in this pro-Israeli country, shocked—as they are—by the actions of extremist suicide bombers in Israel. Recent arrivals often lack educational or occupational skills and are in working-class trades. Others are middle class and not concentrated in urban neighborhoods like their compatriots. Social organizations, like local coffee shops or the national Ramallah Federation, ease the adjustment of the newcomers.

8.   Iranian middle-class professionals, who disliked either the political climate and/or the standard of living in their homeland, first came to the United States either to stay or as temporary sojourners. Ansari identified four types of Iranian immigrants: Persian Yankees, involuntary immigrants, cosmopolitans, and *belataklif* or ambivalent immigrants. The latter live as dually marginal men, emotionally alienated in both countries. Second-generation Iranian Americans, mostly in middle-class professional families, grow up in child-centered, egalitarian families unlike the patriarchal, authoritarian families of their parents' childhood in Iran. U.S. Baha'i, a persecuted minority in Iran, outnumber those still in their homeland.

9.   Iraqis illustrate how homeland conditions are important in determining adjustment patterns in America. Immigrants who arrived prior to World War II exemplify a *gemeinschaft* subsociety that is virtually self-enclosed. Recent arrivals are better educated and more urbanized, and possess an Arab, rather than a village, consciousness. They interact more with outsiders and do not refrain from participating in formal organizations.

10. Turks have not migrated to the United States in substantial numbers because of Turkish restrictions and a tradition opposing small-group migration. The cruelties of the Ottoman Empire directed at Christian Armenians and Syrian-Lebanese caused a negative American attitude toward the Turks, as indicated in their low placement on social-distance scales. Recent immigrants are better educated than their predecessors, since poorly educated laborers tend to migrate to places like Germany to work.

11. Pakistanis are becoming a significant presence, numbering over 93,000 in the 1990 census. Mostly clustering in the New York, Chicago, and Washington, DC metropolitan areas, three in four are craftsmen, service workers, or laborers.

12. Many nonwestern immigrants have the education and job skills to enter the societal mainstream quickly, while those lesser-skilled help fill a population void in urban and ex urban neighborhoods. Early immigrants, often economically exploited, illustrate conflict theory as do the tensions arising between Asians and other U.S. minorities. Social distance is often greater toward nonwesterners, seen as different because of their physical appearance and religions.

CLASS ACTIVITIES

1. A guest speaker from any of the groups discussed in this chapter could inform the class about current settlement patterns and acculturation problems.

2. An Iranian American, perhaps from your faculty, could speak to the class about the problems of societal hostility because of homeland anti-Americanism. Subsequent class discussion could parallel the experiences of such groups as Japanese Americans during World War II and French Americans during the Adams presidency.

3. Divide the class into small discussion groups. Have students exchange views of residential patterning and community life in their hometowns because of the influx of nonwestern immigrants. Were these instances of nativist reaction?

INTERNET RESOURCES

At this book's Web site (http://www.ablongman.com/parrillo), students should select the cover icon, then Chapter 9 to find a variety of links, exercises, and activities pertinent to this content.

MEDIA MATERIALS

"Arab Americans" (2001, Insight Media, 60 minutes)

Presents a student discussion that explores prejudices and stereotypes of people of Arab descent. It shows how Arabs have become the new ethnic villains in American media and folk knowledge and challenges this vilification with facts about the histories and cultural contributions of some of the diverse groups lumped under the Arab-American rubric.

"The Arabs: Who They Are, and Who They Are Not" (1991, Films for the Humanities & Sciences, 30 minutes)

In this program, Bill Moyers and several prominent experts of Arab descent explore how the image of Arabs as religious fanatics was formed. Edward Said, professor of English at Columbia University, discusses the richness, diversity, and distinguished history of the Arab culture. Former United States Senator James Abourezk, and Jack Shaheen, author of *The TV Arab,* discuss the dehumanization of Arabs in the American media.

"Benaat Chicago: Growing Up Arab and Female in Chicago" (1996, Arab Film, 30 minutes)

This video is the result of the directors' year-long collaboration with Arab American teenagers to document their lives growing up on Chicago's southwest side. It addresses stereotypes and racism towards Arabs and Arab women, while showing what makes many Arab Americans proud of their cultural heritage. Thought provoking and insightful, this video is a complex portrayal of a Chicago community often kept invisible.

"Beyond the Veil: Are Iranian Women Rebelling?" (1997, Films for the Humanities & Sciences, 22 minutes)

A female dons the *hijab*—"modest dress—and goes undercover to learn how Iranian women feel about the mandated dress code and their diminished role in Iranian society. Teenage girls flaunt accepted behavioral codes, while morality police roam Teheran streets in search of offenders. *Hijab* advocates—Islamic scholars, a woman doctor, and a female student—discuss the practice within the context of Islamic religious tradition and its social benefits. Career women and others discuss the broader issue of Islam's right to subjugate women by shaping who they are and how they think.

"Conquering America" (1990, Films for the Humanities & Sciences, 30 minutes)

Asian Indian author Bharati Mukhergee discusses with Bill Moyers America's newest immigrants and the building resentment and tensions between our country's various cultures.

"In My Own Skin: The Complexity of Living as Arab in America" (2001, Insight Media, 15 minutes)

> A thought-provoking collection of meditations on issues of identity, race and gender as experienced by a group of five young Arab women living in New York. Filmed in the months following the tragic events of September 11th, this work provides a fascinating and much-needed look at some of the concerns overlooked by the mainstream media.

"Palestinian Portraits" (1987, First Run/Icarus Films, 22 minutes)

> Hundreds of thousands of Palestinians now live and work in the United States. Too often typecast as terrorists or refugees, this program offers a more rounded perspective as expatriate clergy, neurosurgeons, ballet dancers, and university professors discuss their deep-rooted identification with their culture and history. They describe their longing for their homeland and concern for its future, as their stories, photographs, and songs evoke vivid images of orange groves and traditional life left behind.

"Tales From Arab Detroit" (1994, New Day Films, 45 minutes)

> Through personal glimpses of diverse Arab Americans, this film delineates cross-cultural upheaval and generational conflict in both the recent and established immigrant communities, showing how, in spite of assimilation, economic and social discrimination, the life blood of the culture survives in a generation of new storytellers.

Chapter 10

Black Americans

Chapter 10 At-A-Glance

Detailed Outline	Instructor Resources	Print Supplements	Media Supplements	Professor Notes
Sociohistorical Perspective	**Lecture Topics:** Push and Pull Factors that brought Black immigrants to the U.S. Slavery - Involuntary migration.	**Test Bank** **Textbook Review Questions:** #1 & 2	**PowerPoint** **Media:** "By River, By Rail: History of the Black Migration" (1994, Films for the Humanities & Sciences, 22 min.) "Slavery, Society, and Apartheid" (2004, Insight Media, 4 segments, 54 min. each) **www.ablongman.com /parrillo**	
Institutionalized Racism	**Lecture Topic:** Majority group responses: Anti-Black Legislation, Ku Klux Klan.	**Test Bank** **The Ethnic Experience:** How Northerners Differ from Southerners **Textbook Review Questions:** #4	**PowerPoint** **Media:** "Inside the Ku Klux Klan: Faces of Hate" (1999, Films for the Humanities & Sciences, 53 min.) "The Price of Racism" (1996, Films for the Humanities & Sciences, 50 min.) **www.ablongman.com /parrillo**	
The Winds of Change	**Lecture Topics:** The three phases of desegregation	**Test Bank**	**PowerPoint** **Media:** "Racial Integration: America's Long March" (1996, Films for the Humanities &Sciences, 51 min.) **www.ablongman.com /parrillo**	

Urban Unrest	**Lecture Topics:** The 1960s, 1980s and 1992 Riots.	**Test Bank Textbook Review Questions:** #3	**PowerPoint Media:** "American Apartheid" (1995, Films for the Humanities & Sciences, 37 min.) "Black Against Black Prejudice" (1994, Films for the Humanities & Sciences, 28 min.) **www.ablongman.com /parrillo**	
The Bell-Curve Debate	**Lecture Topics:** Early IQ tests. IQ test performance of Blacks versus other groups. **Class Activities:** #2	**Test Bank**	**PowerPoint Media:** "Pride and Prejudice: A History of Black Culture in America" (1994, Insight Media, 28 min.) "Race: The World's Most Dangerous Myth" (1992, RMI Media Productions, 60 min.) **www.ablongman.com /parrillo**	
Language As Prejudice	**Lecture Topics:** The use of words and symbols to create prejudice and discrimination against Black Americans.	**Test Bank**	**PowerPoint Media:** "BaadAssss Cinema: A Bold Look at 70's Blaxploitation Films" (2002, Insight Media, 56 min.) "One Drop Rule" (2001, California Newsreel, 45 min.) **www.ablongman.com /parrillo**	
Social Indicators of Black Progress Race or Class?	**Lecture Topics:** Education, income, occupation, and housing, and social class. **Class Activities:** #3	**Test Bank The Ethnic Experience:** Adjusting to Northern Urban Life **Textbook Review Questions:** #5	**Power Point Media:** "Growing Up African American" (1998, Insight Media, 25 min.) **www.ablongman.com /parrillo**	

African and Afro-Caribbean Immigrants The Haitians The Jamaicans African-Born Americans Cape Verdean Americans	**Lecture Topics:** experiences of new immigrants in the U.S. **Class Activities:** #4	**Test Bank Textbook Review Questions:** #6	**Power Point** **www.ablongman.com /parrillo**	
Black American Assimilation	**Lecture Topics:** Assimilation of U.S.-born African, Afro-Caribbean and African-born Americans. Similarities and Differences between these groups. **Class Activities:** #1	**Test Bank The International Scene:** The Perception of Race in Brazil	**Power Point Media:** "African-American Cultures in the U.S.A.: Part One and Part Two (1992, RMI Media Productions, 60 min. each) "African-American Leaders of the 20th Century" (2002, Insight Media, 40 min.) "African Americans" (2001, Insight Media, 2 segments, 60 min. each) "America Beyond the Color Line With Henry Louis Gates, Jr." (2003, Insight Media, 220 min.) **www.ablongman.com /parrillo**	
Sociological Analysis Functionalist View Conflict View Interactionist View	**Lecture Topics:** Compare and contrast the three main theoretical views of immigration and acculturation.	**Test Bank Textbook Review Questions:** #7	**PowerPoint** **www.ablongman.com /parrillo**	

CHAPTER 10

BLACK AMERICANS

LEARNING OBJECTIVES

1. To examine the African American experience in relation to the experiences of other racial and ethnic groups, showing how racism and various patterns of majority-minority behavior are more universal

2. To discuss the long-lasting impact of social conditioning and the changes wrought by the civil rights movement

3. To analyze African American progress through the use of the social indicators of education, income, and occupation

4. To examine the black immigrant experience and how cultural differences contribute to increased diversity among black Americans

SUMMARY

1. Forced immigration and enslavement of African Americans negated any cultural insulation or use of social institutions to achieve upward mobility or assimilation. The ideology of racism arose and it shaped values and attitudes long after the end of slavery.

2. Despite advances made by the post-Civil War generation of African Americans, the passage of Jim Crow laws after the turn of the century returned them to a formalized subservient position in society. Jim Crow laws and poor economic conditions served as "push" factors encouraging migration to the North. Labor union hostility, race riots, discrimination in jobs and housing, and *de facto* segregation were the result.

3. By the 1920s the Ku Klux Klan had returned to power, adopting a multi-xenophobic position against Catholics, Jews, foreigners, and African Americans. Its claim then of 3 million members in virtually every state is testimony to the perceived threat of these minority groups among native-born Americans. The KKK remains active today, whether visible in America's trouble spots or hidden in backwoods paramilitary camps.

4. Just as values and attitudes had shifted fifty years earlier with the Jim Crow laws, so they did again. The landmark desegregation ruling in 1954 followed by boycotts, sit-ins, freedom rides, and marches led to the massive civil rights legislation of the mid-1960s. Thus, dramatic changes took place in the opportunities made available to all minorities, but particularly this largest minority group of all.

5. As the civil rights movement gained momentum and spread northward, increased expectations led to increased frustrations. Urban riots in the 1960s, 1980s, and more recently in Los Angeles in 1992 (one form of defiance as a minority response pattern) underscored and intensified the problems. The riots typically sparked white flight and the exodus of stores and businesses from the embattled neighbor-hoods. The LA riot prompted the departure of many middle-class minority peoples also, further weakening the neighborhood economy, stability, and potential.

6. Herrstein and Murray's *The Bell Curve* (1994) argued that intelligence best explains wealth, poverty, and social status. A "cognitive elite" passes its genetic advantages on to their children while a low IQ underclass passes on its genetic disadvantages, resulting in such social pathologies as income, illegitimacy, poverty, and welfare dependency. Critics have attacked the book for its selective use of data, methodology, analysis and contradictions. This book's argumentation is a continuation of the old arguments about intelligence testing that once embroiled Shuey, Jensen, and Shockley.

7. Prejudice can be subtly learned, simply from the connotations of words like *white* and *black,* or from institutionalized racism, wherein people are socialized into seeing racist assertions as objective reality.

8. The social indicators of education, income, and occupation help measure black progress since the U.S. Supreme Court ruling of almost half a century ago. The gap in test scores and years of schooling completed has lessened between blacks and whites. In both income and occupational status, progress and regression have occurred. Many Blacks have improved their economic situation while the number of those in poverty has increased with female-headed families as the fastest-growing segment of the population living in poverty. About 56 percent of all black children under 18 live in a single-parent home.

9. A major controversy among black social scientists centers on whether the current social problems of blacks are based on race or class. Wilson argues the bipolarization demonstrates unprecedented opportunities for blacks to achieve upward mobility, but poverty entraps a growing black underclass ill prepared for the high-technology jobs. Willie and Clarke, among others, counter that racism still pervades society, with whites allowing only token entry while retaining actual power, control and wealth.

10. The "racial divide" noted by Tocqueville in 1835 and Myrdal in 1944 still existed in 1992, Hacker noted. D'Souza offered the conservative argument that eliminating affirmative action will ultimately end racism, while Steinberg took the liberal position of the necessity of such programs. Racial group reactions to the O.J. Simpson trial clearly illustrated differences in black-white perceptions.

11. A wide cultural gulf exists between U.S. blacks and recent African immigrants, as partly reflected in their value orientations and social distance from one another. Nigeria, Ethiopia, and Ghana are the leading suppliers of immigrants from Africa.

12. Cape Verdeans vary widely in their physical appearance. Though out-group members view them as black, they do not, and seek a non-black ethnic identity through their "ethnic markers" of language, food, and music. Numbering over 51,000, they are the second largest group from sub-Saharan Africa, with many living in New England. Nigerians constitute the largest group, with about 28 percent in white-collar occupations.

13. Over 157,000 Haitians entered the United States in the 1990s. Homeland conditions make continued large-scale immigration likely. Most are Roman Catholic, are socially isolated, and have an unemployment rate four times the national average. They live mostly in Florida and New York.

14. Jamaicans are the largest non-Hispanic group from the Caribbean. Most live on the East Coast in urban environments, and give some indication that the second generation is assimilating as black Americans.

15. Given the diversity in culture and length of residence of black Americans, their assimilation varies greatly, even without considering the issue of race. Black culture is a resilient component of U.S. society, despite cultural assimilation and recent gains in structural assimilation (education, occupation, income, and housing). Parrillo's 2001 study shows both the progress and continuing social distance between the races.

16. The International Scene box offers a comparative analysis of racial classification and perception in Brazil and the United States.

17. Functional theory examines slavery as an effective means in developing the South's agrarian economy and the entrenchment of a continuing system of inequality generations after the Civil War, necessitating societal corrections. Conflict theorists stress the economic exploitation of blacks both in slavery and afterwards, citing the dominant group acting to protect its interests, the internal colonialism model, and the evolving 1960s civil rights movement. Interactionists focus upon stereotyping and social definitions arising out of perceived dissimilarities based on skin color.

CLASS ACTIVITIES

1. If your college has both an African and a black student organization, have a representative from each come to your class to discuss their particular interests and why they are separate organizations.

2. Administration of either the Chitlin' or BITCH test as a simulated "IQ Test" is an effective learning experience in inner-city culture. Write to the author for more information.

3. Recent court rulings on Affirmative Action provide excellent discussion matter, particularly if examined within the race v. class argument. This can be done within small groups or as a full class activity.

4. Using the chalk board, sequentially list dominant patterns (legislative controls, etc.) minority patterns (avoidance, etc.) migration patterns (push-pull, chain migration etc.) and invite class to suggest ways American blacks paralleled immigrant patterns.

INTERNET RESOURCES

At this book's Web site (http://www.ablongman.com/parrillo), students should select the cover icon, then Chapter 10 to find a variety of links, exercises, and activities pertinent to this content.

MEDIA MATERIALS

"African-American Cultures in the U.S.A.: Part One" (1992, RMI Media Productions, 60 minutes)

Examines the changing statistical and demographic data of African Americans and why they differ from other ethnic groups. Also discusses the Afrocentric movement with Molefi Asante, one of its main advocates.

"African American Cultures in the U.S.A.: Part Two" (1992, RMI Media productions, 60 minutes)

Examines the concepts of African history and religion, the impact of African-American images on the media, poor academic performance, and how schools perpetuate the African-American stereotype.

American Apartheid" (1995, Films for the Humanities and Sciences, 37 minutes)

Examines African-American equality in society, and asks if past racial gains are slowly eroding in a new wave of racial disharmony. Covers such issues as continuing community segregation, violence in black communities, substandard minority housing, Louis Farrakhan's Million Man March and differing racial reactions to the O.J. Simpson verdict.

"Black Against Black Prejudice" (1994, Films for the Humanities and Sciences, 28 minutes)

Phil Donahue interviews black victims of black prejudice, as well as Mohammed Naseehu Ali from Ghana, who says black-on-black prejudice is worse in Africa; Kathy Russell and Midge Wilson, co-authors of *The Color Complex;* J. Edward Giles, publisher of *Image* magazine; Donna Stewart, who almost lost her job because she was "too light"; and Paul Parker, who disagrees that blacks are fighting against other blacks to such an extent.

"By River, By Rail: History of the Black Migration" (1994, Films for the Humanities and Sciences, 22 minutes)

In the early 20th century, Blacks moved north in hope of a better life with little more than a prayer and the shirts on their backs. In this program, poet Maya Angelou, NAACP President Kweisi Mfume, and a host or other African-Americans recount the story of the migration, of separated families, and of the hardships, prejudice, and struggle for acceptance in the North that resulted in disillusionment.

"Growing Up African American" (1998, Insight Media, 25 minutes)

Focusing on significant achievements of African Americans in the past three centuries, this video stresses the importance of understanding U.S. culture as the composite achievement of many different people from many diverse backgrounds.

"How Did Race and Racism Get Started?" (2002, Insight Media, 27 minutes)

In this program, Professor Joseph Graves of Arizona State University looks at the evolution of eugenics, Social Darwinism, and theories of racial inferiority. Graves' views are compared to the theories of William Shockley, the physicist who argued that blacks are intellectually inferior to whites.

"Inside the Ku Klux Klan: Faces of Hate" (1999, Films for the Humanities and Sciences, 53 min.)

In this compelling program, the leaders of the American Knights of the KKK and the Invisible Empire of the KKK air their xenophobic views and discuss their efforts to boost membership through rallies, the Internet, and pamphlets. Civil rights crusader Morris Dees, historian David Oshinsky, authors Raphael Ezekiel and Wyn Craig Wade, representatives of the NAACP and the Anti-Defamation League, and religious and civic leaders analyze the Klan's ideology and deflate their rhetoric. Riveting footage of Klan rallies is included. Contains inflammatory language

"One Drop Rule" (2001, California Newsreel, 45 minutes)

What makes someone black? Is it "one drop of blood," a way of speaking and dressing? Examines experiences of lighter- and darker-skinned African Americans, and explores issues of interracial dating and marriages, biracial children and their difficulties.

"The Price of Racism" (1996, Films for the Humanities and Sciences, 50 minutes)

Vividly portrays the mindless ugliness and irrevocable consequences of racism through five cases in which racism led to violence. Each act destroyed not only its victim, but others as well including the perpetrator, and left in its wake a string of broken lives, strained marriages, financial ruin, traumatized adults and children.

"Pride and Prejudice: A History of Black Culture in America" (1994, Insight Media, 28 minutes)

This program examines the intellectual, artistic, and cultural contributions of African Americans to U.S. society.

"Race: The World's Most Dangerous Myth" (1992, RMI Media Productions, 60 minutes)

The concept of race examined from a scientific and cultural perspective. Also covers classifications of race and a Racial Quotient Questionnaire.

"Racial Integration: America's Long March" (1996, Films for the Humanities and Sciences, 51 minutes)

Gives an informative journey through the U.S. civil rights movement and then a look at the current status of integration and race relations. Included are southern reaction to the Voting Rights Act of 1965, a white Chicago mob stoning the late Martin Luther King, Jr., Alabama Gov. George Wallace's segregationist political movement, Jesse Jackson's presidential campaigns, and the 1992 Los Angeles riot.

Chapter 11
Hispanic Americans

Chapter 11 At-A-Glance

Detailed Outline	Instructor Resources	Print Supplements	Media Supplements	Professor Notes
Sociohistorical Perspective	**Lecture Topics:** Early push and pull factors that led to various Hispanic groups immigrating to the U.S.	Test Bank	PowerPoint **www.ablongman.com/ parrillo**	
Hispanic Culture Cultural Differentiation Racial Attitudes Other Cultural Attributes	**Lecture Topic:** Cultural beliefs and practices differ between Hispanic groups based on urbanization, amount of outside contact, and social class. **Class Activities:** #3	Test Bank **The International Scene:** Cultural Diffusion in Argentina **Textbook Review Questions: #1**	PowerPoint **Media:** "Celebrating Cinco de Mayo" (2003, Insight Media, 20 min.) "Hispanic Americans: One or Many Cultures?" (1995, Films for the Humanities & Sciences, 44 min.) **www.ablongman.com/ parrillo**	
Social Indicators of Hispanic Progress Education Income Occupation	**Lecture Topics:** Data reflecting Hispanic progress in some areas of education, income, and occupation.	Test Bank **Textbook Review Questions: #2 & 3**	PowerPoint **Media:** "The Bronze Screen: 100 Years of the Latino Image in Hollywood" (2002, Insight Media, 88 min.) "The Status of Latina Women" (1991, Films for the Humanities & Sciences, 26 min.) **www.ablongman.com/ parrillo**	

Hispanic Immigrant Groups The Mexicans The Puerto Ricans The Cubans The Carribbean, Central, and South Americans	**Lecture Topics:** Immigrant early experiences. Majority and minority group responses to Hispanic immigration. **Class Activities:** #1	**Test Bank** **The Ethnic Experience:** Harassment Against Early Migrants **The Ethnic Experience:** Brotherhood in Talk and in Deed **Textbook Review Questions:** #4, 5 & 6	**PowerPoint** **Media:** "The American Dream: Puerto Ricans and Mexicans in New York" (2003, Insight Media, 30 min.) "Hispanic Americans" (1993, Insight Media, 3 volumes, 30 min. each) "My American Girls: A Dominican Story" (2001 Filmakers Library, 62 min.) "Ties That Bind: Immigration Stories" (1996, Films for the Humanities & Sciences, 56 min.) "Violence By and Against Latinos" (1990, Films for the Humanities & Sciences, 28 min.) **www.ablongman.com/ parrillo**	
Hispanic American Assimilation	**Lecture Topics:** Cultural pluralism of Hispanic Americans. **Class Activites:** #2	**Test Bank** **The Ethnic Experience:** Cultural Traits and Adjustment.	**Power Point** **Media:** "The Blending of Culture: Latino Influence on the United States" (2001, Films for the Humanities & Sciences, 30 min.) "Biculturism and Acculturation among Latinos" (1991, Films for the Humanities & Sciences, 28 min.) "Hispanic-American Cultures in the U.S.A." (1992, RMI Media Productions, 60 min.) "Understanding Our Differences: Mexicans and Americans" (1998, Insight Media, 25 min.) **www.ablongman.com/ parrillo**	

Sociological Analysis	Lecture Topics:	Test Bank	PowerPoint	
Functionalist View Conflict View Interactionist View	Compare and contrast the three main theoretical views of immigration and acculturation.		www.ablongman.com/ parrillo	

CHAPTER 11

HISPANIC AMERICANS

LEARNING OBJECTIVES

1. To study the Hispanic experience in the United States from a sociohistorical perspective

2. To make students aware of the great diversity among the various Hispanic groups and within specific groups, such as the Mexicans

3. To analyze the present socioeconomic status of the major Hispanic groups and some of the reasons for the differences

4. To understand current assimilation patterns among various Hispanic groups and the ongoing cultural pluralism in their communities

SUMMARY

1. The Hispanic experience varies greatly, depending upon ethnic group, area of settlement, and time period. The agricultural needs of the Southwest and the industrial needs of the East, for example, have affected adjustment, acceptance, and acculturation. For most, overpopulation and poor economic conditions are important "push" factors in migration.

2. Although distinct by nationality and culture, some common bonds exist among Hispanics besides their language. In varying degrees, many subscribe to the concepts of *La Raza Cosmica, machismo* and *marianismo,* and *dignidad.* Because skin color is less important than social class as an indicator of status, racial discrimination is an unexpected experience for most Latinos. Other cultural differences exist, including attitudes about time, pace, and physical proximity.

3. The Hispanic population in the United States is a rapidly growing minority because of a high birth rate, low average age, and high migration rate. Spanish is the second most common language spoken in the United States. Physical and psychological proximity to their homelands, continuing large-scale migrations, endogamy, and less societal pressures for assimilation help reinforce cultural pluralism in the subcommunities.

4. The International Scene box describes the cultural diffusion in Argentina that permeates everyday life and reflects a more distinct European orientation than other Latin American countries.

5. A larger percentage of Hispanics than non-Hispanics are young, reflecting a higher fertility rate and the high percentage of young adult immigrants. Although there is wide diversity among the various Hispanic groups, the data on educational attainment and school dropouts show a lagging behind both non-Hispanic whites and blacks. However, Hispanics fare slightly better than black in higher incomes and a lower poverty rate.

6. Although diverse in terms of assimilation and socioeconomic status, most Mexican Americans today are extremely poor, whether they live in urban or rural areas. Leaving an impoverished land for the economic opportunities to the north, they found their reception varying with the fluctuating demand for labor. Government efforts at expulsion in the 1930s and 1950s—times of economic trouble—and the Zoot Suit Riots of 1943 are examples of power and hostility directed against the Mexican Americans. Fighting stereotyping and overcrowded housing in the segregated poor sections of smaller cities and towns throughout the Southwest, some Chicanos have attempted to restore pride among their people through social or political action, with limited results. Problems of high unemployment, low skills, and education, and the continual flow of illegal aliens remain, as do problems of stereotyping because of illegal aliens and youth gangs in urban barrios.

7. Overpopulation, economic opportunities on the mainland, and their status as United States nationals were the primary "push-pull" factors in Puerto Rican migration. Their frequent shuttle-migration patterns curtailed as strong a development of community life as earlier immigrants had established. Lack of a strong ethnic church, coupled with structural blue-collar unemployment, and racial discrimination, helps explain the poverty and lack of cohesiveness in many Puerto Rican neighborhoods. Changes visible among the second generation are activist organizations and collective community efforts regarding education, welfare, antipoverty programs, and housing. Also, Hispanic churches are now taking a more active role in the community.

8. Compared to Mexican Americans, Puerto Ricans are less likely to have arrived recently, be better educated and more fluent in English and, if employed, earning more money. Yet few Mexican Americans live in poverty and, if they do, are less likely to seek government assistance than the Puerto Rican poor. Differences in unionized or non-unionized labor markets, in northern central cities and southwestern economic conditions, and in the number of female-headed families help explain the contrast.

9. Although Cuban communities in the United States date back to 1850, most Cuban immigrants have been refugees fleeing the Castro regime since the late 1950s. Cuban arrivals up to 1980 were mostly middle class with high education levels and marketable job skills; they quickly achieved socioeconomic status closer to the total United States population and higher than any other Hispanic group. The largest single influx of Cubans was the 125,000 on the Mariel boatlift in 1980 who were mostly working or lower class. The Cuban-American population is now over 1.2 million. Cuban cultural values emphasize avoidance of being a *tacaño* (cheapskate) and *pesado* (disagreeable person)

10. Overpopulation, economic hardship, and political turmoil have generated significant increases from several Central and South American countries. Over 717,000 Dominicans have arrived since 1971. Two out of three live in New York State, often in distinctive urban neighborhoods alongside Puerto Ricans. Many are unskilled and live in poverty. Salvadorans, numbering well over 655,000, are mostly refugees from the violence in their homeland. Many came as illegals through the sanctuary movement. Nicaraguans also came as refugees, first a middle class wave and then the peasants. Over 177,000 now reside in the United States, many concentrated in Florida and southern California. Over 470,000 Colombians are a mixture of educated professionals and low-skilled peasants and live mostly in urban areas. They suffer from a negative stereotype because of the drug cartel.

11. The diversity among Hispanic groups also affects their assimilation. With education as a key indicator, the high attrition rate of immigrant youths is of great concern. Intermarriage with non-Hispanics is increasing, as it is among different national-origin Hispanics.

12. Functional analysis stresses: (1) development of supportive ethnic communities and political power from the rapid Hispanic population growth; (2) existence of a dual economy, and (3) the system's inability to absorb so many that quickly. Conflict theorists emphasize the internal colonialism model, exploitation of migrant workers and sweatshop employees, and the growing protest movements to overcome the power differential. Interactionists consider (1) misperceptions of Hispanic diversity and culture, and (2) public unawareness of Hispanic-American patterns as repetitive of earlier immigrants.

CLASS ACTIVITIES

1. Depending upon your locale, a guest speaker from the local police or public school system could discuss institutional responses to the growing Hispanic population and any concomitant problems.

2. A representative from a Hispanic organization could tell the class of its purpose, efforts, and the acculturation patterns of its people.

3. Among the many topics that Hispanic students in your class or college could share with the group are: religious practices here and in their homeland, teenage dating, language difficulties, and other acculturation concerns.

INTERNET RESOURCES

At this book's Web site (http://www.ablongman.com/parrillo), students should select the cover icon, then Chapter 11 to find a variety of links, exercises, and activities pertinent to this content.

MEDIA MATERIALS

"The American Dream: Puerto Ricans and Mexicans in New York" (2003, Insight Media, 30 minutes)

This program focuses on the Latino experience in New York City, particularly in the Bronx. It discusses the Spanish-speaking infrastructure and leadership of the Puerto Rican community and looks at the efforts of the Mexican immigrant population's struggle as undocumented workers. The program highlights the similarities and differences between the two groups.

"The Blending of Culture: Latino Influence on the United States" (2001, Films for the Humanities & Sciences, 30 minutes)

Looks at the "Three Houses of Latino Culture"—Cuban, Puerto Rican, and Mexican-American—and their widespread influence from entertainment to politics to economics. Key issues include how long Hispanics have been in America and how U.S. immigration laws affect their assimilation. Interviews with Latino community leaders—university presidents, professors, artists, doctors, CEOs, bishops, and ministers—bring home the diversity and achievement of this rapidly expanding segment of the American populace.

"Biculturalism and Acculturation among Latinos" (1991, Films for the Humanities & Sciences, 28 minutes)

As Latinos struggle with pressures to reaffirm their heritage, they also face pressures to assimilate. This program examines those choices, explores misperceptions about who are the U.S. Latinos, and probes the relationship between ethnic identity and entrepreneurial success in the U.S. marketplace.

"The Bronze Screen: 100 Years of the Latino Image in Hollywood" (2002, Insight Media, 88 minutes)

This program traces the progression of Latino stereotypes in Hollywood films. The DVD includes film tributes to Anthony Quinn, Rita Hayworth, and Rita Moreno.

"Celebrating Cinco de Mayo" (2003, Insight Media, 20 minutes)

> Parades, traditional foods, and colorful crafts are hallmarks of Cinco de Mayo. This video explores the traditions and significance of the holiday, which glorifies freedom and liberty, and shows how Cinco de Mayo provides the United States and Mexico with the annual opportunity to acknowledge and reaffirm their friendship.

"Hispanic Americans" (1993, Insight Media, 3 volumes, 30 minutes each)

> This set of videos celebrates the cultural heritage of Central, Mexican, and Puerto Rican Americans. Examines traditions of each group, when and why each immigrated, and explores how they have preserved their cultural identities.

"Hispanic-American Cultures in the U.S.A." (1992, RMI Media Productions, 60 minutes)

> This program discusses the multiple ethnic groups classified as Hispanics, as well as the issues of bilingualism and color in Hispanic society.

"Hispanic Americans: One or Many Cultures?" (1995, Films for the Humanities & Sciences, 44 minutes)

> Three Hispanic Americans—a Puerto Rican New York judge, a Cuban-born former mayor of Miami, and a Mexican restaurateur—discuss what unites and divides their ethnic groups, group self-perceptions, problems related to Mexican immigration in California and the power of voting to achieve common goals.

"My American Girls: A Dominican Story" (2001, Filmmakers Library, 62 minutes)

> Captures the immigrant experience with a vivid portrayal of a Dominican family living in Brooklyn. The bittersweet contradictions between generations form the core of the film as we watch a family sort out the rewards and costs of pursuing the American dream.

"The Status of Latina Women" (1991, Films for the Humanities & Sciences, 26 minutes)

> Compares differences between U.S. Latinas and their Latin American and North American counterparts. Also examines how Latin men view successful women, and the myths and mystique of machismo in an age of two-career families.

"Ties That Bind: Immigration Stories" (1996, Films for the Humanities & Sciences, 56 minutes)

This program roams both sides of the Texas-Mexico border, exploring the root causes of why Mexicans immigrate. The role played by transnational corporations and their social and economic impact on both Mexicans and other North Americans is considered. Other segments explore the determination of immigrants and restrictive immigration policies; the strong family values immigrants bring with them as a positive impact on U.S. culture; and immigrant organizations within the context of the American citizen action tradition.

"Understanding Our Differences: Mexicans and Americans" (1998, Insight Media, 25 minutes)

Examines the perceived cultural differences between Mexicans and Americans that often spark mutual conflict and distrust. It explores the experiences of two neighboring families, the Petersons and the Garcias, as they confront real-world questions and common misconceptions about each other. Includes teenage discussion on stereotyping.

"Violence By and Against Latinos" (1990, Films for the Humanities & Sciences, 28 minutes)

This program looks at a drive-by shooting, counseling efforts for school-age victims, the effects of the LA riots on various immigrant groups and the African-American community, and violence against Latina women in their homes.

Chapter 12

Religious Minorities

Chapter 12 At-A-Glance

Detailed Outline	Instructor Resources	Print Supplements	Media Supplements	Professor Notes
Sociohistorical Perspective	**Lecture Topics:** The significance of religion for almost all immigration groups.	Test Bank	**PowerPoint Media:** "Religion" (1991, Insight Media, 30 min.) "Sacred Text and Stories" (1998, Films for the Humanities & Sciences, 21 min.) **www.ablongman.com /parrillo**	
Religious Denominations Catholic Americans Jewish Americans The Mormons Muslim Americans The Amish The Rastafarians The Santerians Hindu Americans	**Lecture Topic:** Religious beliefs and values of each religion. Minority and majority group responses to the religions of various immigrant groups. **Class Activities: #1 & 3**	**Test Bank The Ethnic Experience:** My American Dream **The Ethnic Experience:** A Muslim Among Christians **The Internation Scene:** Religious Diversity in Israel **Textbook Review Questions: #1 - 8**	**PowerPoint Media:** "African American Religions: The Nation of Islam" (1994, RMI Media Productions, 60 min.) "Hinduism: Elephant God" (1996, Films for the Humanities & Sciences, 15 min.) "Islam: Sacrifice to Allah" (1996, Films for the Humanities & Sciences, 15 min.) "Judaism: Bar Mitzvah Boys" (1996, Films for the Humanities & Sciences, 15 min.) "A Laugh, a Tear, a Mitzvah" (1998, PBS, 57 min.) "Moslems in America" (1997, Insight Media, 23 min.) "Pentecostalism: Caribbean Christmas" (1996, Films for the Humanities & Sciences, 15 min.) "Roman Catholicism:	

			Flowers in May" (1996, Films for the Humanities & Sciences, 15 min.) "Sikhism: The Golden Temple" (1996, Films for the Humanities & Sciences, 21 min.) **www.ablongman.com /parrillo**	
Religion and U.S.. Society	**Lecture Topics:** current controversies: separation of church and state; abortion; and creationism. Religious assimilation. **Class Activities:** #2	**Test Bank Textbook Review Questions:** #9	**PowerPoint** "Religion and Politics in American Culture" (1994, RMI Media Productions, 60 min.) "Women in Islam" (1997, Insight Media, 60 min.) **www.ablongman.com /parrillo**	
Sociological Analysis Functionalist View Conflict View Interactionist View	**Lecture Topics:** Compare and contrast the three main theoretical views of immigration and acculturation.	**Test Bank Textbook Review Questions:** 10	**PowerPoint** **www.ablongman.com /parrillo**	

CHAPTER 12

RELIGIOUS MINORITIES

LEARNING OBJECTIVES

1. To examine the role of religion as an important component in the study of minorities

2. To study the U.S. interaction experiences of Catholics, Jews, Mormons, Muslims, Amish, Rastafarians, Santerians, and Hindus.

3. To discuss religion as an aspect of contemporary American culture, including current controversies

4. To apply the three major sociological perspectives to religious intergroup relations in the United States

SUMMARY

1. Long the refuge of religious groups fleeing persecution, the United States has maintained from its beginnings two fundamental principles: freedom of religion and separation of church and state. Religion serves as a unifying bond for many groups, often as a significant center of immigrant communities. Religion has also frequently been a source of conflict, as bigotry and intolerance caused suffering and hardship to some religious minorities.

2. Catholic Americans, first mostly among Germans and Irish immigrants, experienced intense societal hostility throughout much of the 19th century. In the early 20th century, nativist actions continued, particularly through the Ku Klux Klan. Primary sources of conflict were Protestant concerns of papal domination and indoctrination, especially the parochial school system, which they saw as propagating "ignorance and superstition." Roman Catholics today are the largest single religious denomination in the country; they are found in all occupations and in many leadership roles. Catholic views on abortion, birth control, pornography, and school prayer tend to parallel those of conservative Protestants.

3. Sephardic Jewish immigrants experienced some discrimination but substantial assimilation from colonial times to the mid-nineteenth century when substantial numbers of German Jews emigrated, especially between 1880 and 1920, when anti-Semitism became more pronounced. Their job skills, educational values, and family migrations combined to enable many, but not all, Jewish people to achieve upward mobility more rapidly than most other ethnic groups. Social ostracism, however, hindered their structural assimilation. As in many Christian ethnic communities, the Jewish religious institution—the synagogue—

played a significant role in the community structure. A 1990 study commissioned by the Council of Jewish Federations revealed a 52 percent intermarriage rate among American Jews, with only 28 percent of the children in these marriages raised in the Jewish faith. Coupled with a low birthrate and Jewish immigration, these patterns have led to both pessimistic and optimistic scenarios about the future of Judaism in the United States.

4. The International Scene box profiles the extensive religious diversity in Israel, allowing for discussion on stereotyping, perceptions, and reality.

5. Harassment, violence, murder, and expulsion confronted the Mormons in their early years of existence, ultimately prompting an avoidance response of migration to Utah. There, tens of thousands of European immigrant converts joined them to build a highly successful religious community. Following a short war challenging their theocratic political power and legislation forbidding their polygamous marriages, the Mormons became a prosperous and accepted church group. An emphasis on family togetherness, educational achievement, missionary work, and economic welfare mark their social institutions. Overcoming charges of racism by revision of church doctrine to permit Blacks in the priesthood, Mormons have recently been criticized as sexist, since women are not permitted to be part of the church hierarchy.

6. Islam encompasses many diverse peoples, not just Arabs. Muslim Americans now exceed four million and over 1,400 mosques now pepper the American landscape. Islam is a conservative faith strictly following the *Shai'ah,* based on teachings from the *Koran,* which incorporates many of the beliefs and practices of the Jewish and Christian faiths.

7. The Amish, a branch of the Mennonites, live in highly integrated communities in several states. Clothing, physical appearance, language, and behavioral norms reinforce their group identity and cohesiveness. Permitting some degree of adolescent rebellion before adult baptisms and endogamous marriages helps preserve a low attrition rate among them. Some conflicts with government regulations have occurred, though most have been resolved. The Amish birth rate, ingroup solidarity, and resistance to outside influences suggests they will continue to remain a persistent subculture.

8. Jamaican-American Rastafarians offer a striking physical appearance, with values and practices also making them quite distinguishable from other groups. They have encountered hostility and harassment both in Jamaica and the United States, though they themselves seek no confrontations. Their hairstyle, language, avoidance of all chemically processed goods or foods, and fondness for marijuana are their predominant attributes. They are a highly adaptive, mostly low-income people, whose numbers are growing due to increased immigration from Jamaica.

9. Santería came to the United States from Cuba, where it has flourished since the 17th century when brought there by West African slaves. Prohibited from practicing their religion openly, the slaves hid much of their religion behind a facade of Catholicism. Now attracting many non-Cubans, black and white alike, it has metamorphosed into a less ethnocentric religion, even blending in some Puerto Rican spiritism. Trance possession, symbolism, and sacrificial offerings are integral parts or this faith. Animal rights activists and public officials have sought bans against the animal sacrifices. Estimates place U.S. practitioners between 500,000 and one million.

10. Hinduism, the world's third largest religion, lacks a single founder, specific theological system or religious organization. Not strictly a religion, a Hindu practitioner can also be devout in another faith. Hindus consider cow slaughter a sacrilege and believe reincarnation, based on past good or bad acts, causes rebirth at a higher or lower level and explains the unequal distribution of wealth, prestige, or suffering. Among the more than one million U.S. Hindus, mostly Asian Indians, immigrant parents want their children to learn Hindu values and beliefs, but few want them to perform traditional Hindu rituals or necessarily marry another Hindu. Second-generation Americans typically view Hinduism more as a social religion.

11. Although we are a more secular society today, religion remains an important factor in millions of Americans' lives. Nine in ten Americans believes in God; about half belong to a church, temple, or synagogue; and nearly half attend a weekly worship service. Religion continues to stir controversies on such subjects as abortion, evolution, and school prayer.

12 Religious assimilation depends heavily on prevailing societal attitudes, degree of dissimilarity, and length of residence. Past examples of Baptists, Catholics, and Jews are given, though they are now all mainstream. Perhaps one aftermath of nine-eleven may be an accelerated assimilation of Muslim Americans, similar to the Japanese in World War II.

13. Functional analysis sees religion as a social cement, unifying a people and offering a buttress against stress and troubles. Conflict analysis probes religious bigotry for underlying struggles for political or economic power. Interactionist analysis looks at societal labeling and intragroup cooperative interpretation.

CLASS ACTIVITIES

1. An in-class survey of its religious composition could reveal resource persons for augmenting text material or initiating discussion on religious similarities and dissimilarities, and accommodation needs. For example, what of Sunday "blue" laws for those whose Sabbath is Friday or Saturday, or who have different religious holy days?

2. The separation of church and state becomes a volatile issue when applied to such controversial issues as public Nativity displays, school prayers, aid to parochial schools, or abortion. Provocative class-wide or small group discussion can ensue from properly motivated topic presentations.

3. Student acceptance of the constitutional guarantee of freedom of religion might be tested by presenting case histories about alleged brainwashing of "Moonies", airport solicitations by Hari Krishna members, and the like. The key here is to illustrate some practices outside the norm, generate some negative observations if possible, and compare to past societal responses to religious groups discussed in this chapter.

INTERNET RESOURCES

At this book's Web site (http://www.ablongman.com/parrillo), students should select the cover icon, then Chapter 12 to find a variety of links, exercises, and activities pertinent to this content.

MEDIA MATERIALS

"African American Religions: The Nation of Islam" (1994, RMI Media Productions, 60 minutes)

Examines African-American sectarianism in the 20th century, with historical background on the Nation of Islam, the roles of Elijah Muhammed, Malcolm X, and Louis Farrakkan, and conflict with European American culture core.

"Hinduism: Elephant God" (1996, Films for the Humanities & Sciences, 15 minutes)

Provides an overview of Hinduism, the world's oldest religion, and examines the rites and rituals of the Ganesh Festival. Held in honor of the Hindu elephant god of good fortune, one of Hinduism's most important deities, it is the highlight of the Hindu religious year. Hindu children discuss the significance of the festival—its symbols, rituals, such as the holy fire, ceremonial foods, and the communities involvement in the celebration.

"Islam: Sacrifice to Allah" (1996, Films for the Humanities & Sciences, 15 minutes)

Traces the historical roots and many of the rituals of the Muslim faith, including the Eid-ul Adha festival commemorating the prophet Abraham's sacrifice of a ram at the command of God. The five pillars of Islam—belief in one God, prayer, charity, fasting, and pilgrimage to Mecca—are discussed as major tenets of the faith. Various rituals are examined, including the symbolic sharing of a slain ram's meat with the poor.

"Judaism: Bar Mitzvah Boys" (1996, Films for the Humanities & Sciences, 15 minutes)

In Jerusalem, a 13 year-old boy is bar mitzvahed—the ceremony, or rite of passage, that allows young Jewish males to participate fully in their religion. The symbolism of both the ceremony and sacred objects, such as the prayer shawl, is explained. Other topics include the significance of the Torah and the Talmud.

"A Laugh, a Tear, a Mitzvah" (1998, PBS, 57 minutes)

Explores the dynamic evolution of the legacy of Jewish identity in the United States and offers a glimpse of how Jewish immigrant communities assimilated and achieved success. It brings alive the spirit and determination of a group of Americans who have overcome hardship, bigotry, and adversity and contributed to the United States.

"Moslems in America" (1997, Insight Media, 23 minutes)

Examines not only the tenets of the Moslem faith, but also the stereotypes of Moslems and the American tendency to jump to conclusions regarding Moslem responsibility for terrorist acts. Includes candid discussions of several Moslems about their U.S. cultural identity.

"Pentecostalism: Caribbean Christmas" (1996, Films for the Humanities & Sciences, 15 minutes)

Focuses on Pentecostal Christmas celebrations on Barbados, where a young convert to the religion talks about its basic precepts and its influence on her life. Scenes shot at services feature lively hymns and the practice of "speaking in tongues," which adherents believe is communication between church members and God.

"Religion" (1991, Insight Media, 30 minutes)

Using examples from several major religions, this program shows the various functions of religion and how it reflects a society's values. Analyzes religion as a social structure, religiosity in the United States and contemporary trends in religion.

"Religion and Politics in American Culture" (1994, RMI Media Productions, 60 minutes)

Key Supreme Court cases regarding religion and the public sphere are discussed. Covers the free exercise of religion, the establishment of religion, and religion and politics in U.S. culture.

"Roman Catholicism: Flowers in May" (1996, Films for the Humanities & Sciences, 15 minutes)

Explains the significance of the Flores de Mayo Festival and the importance of the Virgin Mary to Filipino Catholics. It also describes how the religion came to the islands via the Spaniards in the 17th century, and illustrates its influence on the lives of the people. The importance of the Pope and the significance of various rituals connected with the faith are explained, including the Mass, Confession, and Holy Communion. Religion is incorporated into the everyday lives of teens through a local religious group.

"Sacred Text and Stories" (1998, Films for the Humanities & Sciences, 21 minutes)

Examines and analyzes the significance of the religious documents of the five major religions—the Christian Bible, The Hebrew Torah, the Islamic Koran, the Hindu Veda, and the Buddhist sutras. Discusses the similarities among the texts—how the documents keep traditions alive, connect the past to the present, and preserve their religion for future generations. Also documents the lives and teachings of the founding fathers of the Mormon religion that play important roles in unifying believers.

"Sikhism: The Golden Temple" (1996, Films for the Humanities & Sciences, 15 minutes)

This program traces the roots of Sikhism from its founder Guru Nanak in 1469 through today. Discusses Sikhism's central precepts—belief in one God, the equality of all people, sharing, and the performance of good deeds—within the context of daily life.

"Women in Islam" (1997, Insight Media, 60 minutes)

In an interview with law professor Azizah Al-Hibri focusing on women in Islam, this video addresses cultural issues, traditional values, questions raised by modernization, and issues about Shariah.

Chapter 13

Women As A Minority Group

Chapter 13 At-A-Glance

Detailed Outline	Instructor Resources	Print Supplements	Media Supplements	Professor Notes
Sociohistorical Perspective	**Lecture Topics:** Sexism as an ideology; Historical writings about the status of women (Freud, Myrdal, Hacker, Friedman). **Class Activities: #1**	Test Bank	**PowerPoint Media:** "Novelists, Playwrights, Poets" (2003, Insight Media) "Sexual Stereotypes in the Media" (2001, Insight Media, 25 min.) **www.ablongman.com/par rillo**	
Restrictions on Women Male dominance Sexual Property Suffrage	**Lecture Topic:** Discrimination against women, lack of rights, minority status.	**Test Bank The Gender Experience:** An Early Plea for Equal Rights **Textbook Review Questions: #1, 2, 4**	**PowerPoint Media:** "Facing Diversity: Responding to Violence Against Women From Diverse Cultures" (2001, 40 min.) "Oil and Water: The Truth About Rape" (2003, Insight Media, 35 min.) "Sex, Murder, and Video Games" (2003, Insight Media, 15 min.) **www.ablongman.com/par rillo**	
The Realities of Sexual Differences Biological Socialization and Gender Roles	**Lecture Topics:** The nature versus nurture debate as it applies to sexual differences - real or imagined.	**Test Bank The Gender Experience:** A Feminist's List of "Barbarous Rituals" **Textbook Review Questions: #3**	**PowerPoint Media:** Gender Socialization" (1993, Insight Media, 60 min.) "Masai Woment" (2004, Insight Media, 55 min.) "Monuments Are for Men, Waffles Are for Women: Gender Permanence and Impermanence" (2000, University of California, 32 min.) "Playing (Un)Fair" (2002, Insight Media, 30 min.) **www.ablongman.com/par rillo**	

Immigrant and Minority Women Vestiges of White Ethnic Orientations Today's Minority Women	**Lecture Topics:** The Women's Liberation Movement overlooks women of color. The double-minority issue: women of color. **Class Activities:** #3	**Test Bank**	**PowerPoint** **Media:** "The Changing Role of Hispanic Women" (1998, Films for the Humanities & Sciences, 44 min.) "Daughters of Afghanistan" (2004, Insight Media, 58 min.) "Is Feminism Dead?" (1999, Films for the Humanities & Sciences, 29 min.) **www.ablongman.com/par rillo**
Social Indicators of Women's Status Education Income Occupation	**Lecture Topics:** Women earn 69 cents for every dollar earned by men. Women still earn less than men in almost every field, including those dominated by women. **Class Activities:** #2 &4	**Test Bank** **The International Scene:** Women's Status in Canada **The International Scene:** Women's Changing Status in Japan **Textbook Review Questions:** #5	**Power Point** **Media:** "Beyond the Glass Ceiling"(1992, Teacher's Video Company, 41 min.) "Career Choice" (1994, RMI Media Productions, 60 min.) "The Double Shift" (1996, Films for the Humanities & Sciences, 47 min.) "Shattering the Glass Ceiling" (1999, Insight Media, 30 min.) "Women in the Workplace" (1998, Insight Media, 20 min.) **www.ablongman.com/par rillo**
Sexual Harassment The Hill-Thomas Hearings Complaints and Actions **Sexism and the Law**	**Lecture Topics:** Discuss the progress, or lack thereof, that women have made through the courts.	**Test Bank** **Textbook Review Questions:** #6	**PowerPoint** **Media:** "Gender Issues in the U.S.A." (1992, RMI Media Productions, 2 volumes, 60 min. each) "Killing Us Softly 3: Advertising's Image of Women" (1999, Insight Media, 30 min.) **www.ablongman.com/par rillo**
Women and Politics	**Lecture Topics:** The gradual increase in the number of women entering the political arena.	**Test Bank**	**PowerPoint** **Media:** "Women in American Politics" (1992, Insight Media, 60 min.) "Women of Vision" (1999, Insight Media, 80 min.) **www.ablongman.com/par rillo**

Sociological Analysis Functionalist View Conflict View Interactionist View	Lecture Topics: Compare and contrast the three main theoretical views of immigration and acculturation.	Test Bank Textbook Review Questions: #7	PowerPoint www.ablongman.com/par rillo	

CHAPTER 13

WOMEN AS A MINORITY GROUP

LEARNING OBJECTIVES

1. To study women as a minority group

2. To contrast biological fact from social fiction about gender differences

3. To examine the role of ethnicity impacting upon the status of women in U.S. society

4. To examine the social indicators of education, employment, income, legal rights, and political participation for women

SUMMARY

1. Sexism did not arise as a concept until the 1960s, although the suffragette movement and writings of a few social observers identified problems of male domination earlier. Legal restrictions denied women voting rights, property ownership, contract privileges, as well as many other forms of individual independence. The suffragette movement met fierce resistance but succeeded in securing passage of the Nineteenth Amendment in 1919. Thereafter women did not use their political power much to their advantage. World War II brought many women into the workplace, though many left their jobs when the war ended.

2. Men and women are biologically different in size, weight, strength, longevity, pain tolerance, and aggressive behavior. Both longitudinal studies and cross-cultural comparisons show that stereotypical sex role behavior is not linked to sex hormones, but result from society's definitions of gender identity and the internalized sex role behavior resulting from the socialization process. Girls generally play in dyadic groups in a more structured, narrower world while boys play in larger groups, exploring expanded territory on hikes or bikes, requiring adaptive decisions and self-reliance. In addition, role models, television programming and advertising, even computer games and software create socialization inequities between the sexes.

3. Most immigrants come from societies with traditional sex role orientations, which they maintain in their adopted land, often passing on these traditional values to their children who also retain them as adults. Much of working-class America contains second-generation Americans continuing those traditional behavioral patterns. Today's minority women must often combat both sexism and racial or cultural prejudice.

4. The International Scene box profiles change in Canadian women's status, allowing for comparison with U.S. women.

5. Once limited in educational opportunities, women now attain comparable educational levels with men but many disparities exist in the subject fields as traditional male and female occupational areas retain disproportionate sex ratios.

6. The workplace contains differentiations by occupation or even within occupations where high and low status positions exist, reflecting, say critics, the presence of a glass ceiling.

7. Gender pay inequity, even within the same occupation, partly results from choices corporate women must make between the "fast track" (career upward mobility) and the "mommy track," (motherhood time demands). Reliable childcare and flex-time schedules are not always available. Working women also face a "second shift" at home. Female-headed households and subsequent lower family income have created a feminization of poverty, particularly among minorities.

8. Sexual harassment became a public issue in 1976, generating corrective measures to curtail it. In 1991, the televised confirmation hearings for Supreme Court nominee Clarence Thomas educated the public about sexual harassment through charges brought by Anita Hill. Since the 1991 Tailhook scandal, the military has faced accusations of sexual harassment, prompting the Department of Defense to adopt a zero tolerance policy and take swift action on complaints.

9. Many state laws are sexist in their orientation, though change is gradually occurring. Efforts to pass the Equal Rights Amendment, partly intended to eliminate such inequities quickly, did not succeed in its ratification. In 2004, women accounted for 14 senators, 56 congressional representatives, nine governors and 22% of all state legislators.

10. The second International Scene box profiles women's changing status in Japan, allowing for U.S. comparisons.

11. Functionalists say rapid social change makes traditional sex roles obsolete, requiring new definitions and adjustments to meet social expectations and conditions. Conflict theorists see male domination evolving out of changing economic contributions of the two sexes, reinforced by a sexist ideology, and benefiting both males themselves and employers who reap bigger profits by paying women less. Interactionists concentrate on social definitions, shared expectations, and the emerging new male-female interaction patterns.

CLASS ACTIVITIES

1. Erving Goffman's *Gender Advertisements* offers an excellent opportunity for students to examine sexism in media advertising. Have them bring in newspaper/magazine ads to illustrate its continued presence.

2. Have students do a content analysis of prime-time television shows of male-female portrayals (e.g., presence, status, importance, etc.)

3. Have a guest speaker from your women's studies program speak to the class about the women's movement or team teach a class period. With you emphasizing applications of the three major sociological perspectives, this can be a very effective learning experience.

4. An in-class survey of gender major choices, in relation to text material on gender degree recipients and career choices, could launch discussion on the effects of socialization and societal influences on such choices within your class.

INTERNET RESOURCES

At this book's Web site (http://www.ablongman.com/parrillo), students should select the cover icon, then Chapter 13 to find a variety of links, exercises, and activities pertinent to this content.

MEDIA MATERIALS

"Beyond the Glass Ceiling" (1992, Teacher's Video Company, 41 minutes)

CNN produced this program on women in the workplace. Your students will see how women have struggled to rise in corporate America.

"Career Choice" (1994, RMI Media Productions, 60 minutes)

Examines different characteristics of men's and women's work, and explains the complexity of the gender wage gap, with illustrations of average salaries by sex and ethnic groups.

"The Changing Role of Hispanic Women" (1998, Films for the Humanities & Sciences, 44 minutes)

Several prominent Latina women discuss their changing role within the context of Hispanic family values, male *machismo*, and the traditional role of females as the center of family and community life. Actress Jennifer Lopez explains her choice of career over marriage. A psychiatrist and several Hispanic men examine the issue from the male perspective.

"Daughters of Afghanistan" (2004, Insight Media, 58 minutes)

Following the lives of five women from diverse backgrounds, this program exposes the ongoing struggle of women in modern Afghanistan. It features journalist Sally Armstrong as she interviews women such as Sima Simar, who ignored death threats and defied the edicts of the Taliban by providing healthcare and education to women.

"The Double Shift" (1996, Films for the Humanities & Sciences, 47 minutes)

Examines women juggling family and career: a surgeon paying a price in guilt and lower income; a single mother of three who regrets that her daughter must sacrifice her education to help support the family. Experts discuss women's industrial role during World War II, and a "house husband," whose wife works full time, provides a male perspective.

"Facing Diversity: Responding to Violence Against Women From Diverse Cultures" (2001, Insight Media, 40 minutes)

Each year, millions of women who suffer domestic violence in their own countries immigrate to the United States and Canada. This video describes the barriers these women face; illustrates specific, culturally sensitive practices for victim advocates, police officers, and prosecutors; and shows how women learn to obtain relief from violence and navigate the justice and court systems. It includes examples from Hispanic, East Asian, and South Asian cultures.

"Gender Issues in the U.S.A." (1992, RMI Media Productions, 2 volumes, 60 minutes each)

Part one discusses women in the work force, feminism and recent legislative changes. Part two discusses Robert Bly's *Iron John*, men's groups, rites of passage for men and women.

"Gender Socialization" (1993, Insight Media, 60 minutes)

This video discusses how gender socialization affects self-esteem, emotions, behavior, and world view. It examines how social action has influenced gender socialization in the past and what can be done to effect further change.

"Is Feminism Dead?" (1999, Films for the Humanities & Sciences, 29 minutes)

A new generation of women is questioning the meaning and the value of the battles fought by their mothers and grandmothers. Has feminism somehow gone out of style? Patricia Ireland, Phyllis Schlafly, Ellen Goodman, Bell Hooks, and other feminists appraise the current women's movement and discuss its relevance in today's cultural climate.

"Killing Us Softly 3: Advertising's Image of Women" (1999, Insight Media, 30 minutes)

> Produced by Jean Kilbourne, this program questions whether advertising continues to objectify women's bodies, sexualize young girls, infantilize grown women, and use images of male violence against women to sell products.

"Masai Women" (2004, Insight Media, 55 minutes)

> Documenting the customs, social structures, and beliefs of the Masai, this DVD looks at the women of this male-dominated East African tribe. It examines their roles, from childhood through marriage to old age.

"Monuments Are for Men, Waffles Are for Women: Gender Permanence and Impermanence" (2000, University of California, 32 minutes)

> Explores numerous instances of unrecognized but pervasive gender divisions of activity, their causes and consequences. Will prompt lively discussion on the social construction of gender activities and how these patterns of activities are perpetuated in U.S. culture.

"Novelists, Playwrights, Poets" (2003, CD-ROM, Insight Media)

> This program surveys the course of women in literature from the early 18th century. It looks at influential women authors, the development of new and empowering female literary characters, and social commentary by contemporary women.

"Oil and Water: The Truth About Rape" (2003, Insight Media, 35 minutes)

> This video addresses the challenge of placing blame in the aftermath of a rape incident. It uses a metaphor of oil and water to highlight the critical distinction between a woman's so-called burden to protect herself and society's need to blame the rape perpetrator rather than the rape victim.

"Playing (Un)Fair" (2002, Insight Media, 30 minutes)

> This program looks at media representation of female athletes, demonstrating that while men's identities in sports equated with values of courage and strength, the accomplishments of female athletes are framed in much more stereotypical feminine ways.

"Sex, Murder, and Video Games" (2003, Insight Media, 15 minutes)

A response to the graphic depiction of women as sexual objects and victims of brutal violence in some video games, this program explores the relationship between violence and power. It examines the promotion of violence against women and the pairing of misogynistic violence with entertainment.

"Sexual Stereotypes in Media" (2001, Insight Media, 25 minutes)

Investigates media influence on social and personal views of sexuality; the deliberate use of sexual stereotypes in print media, on television, and in advertising; and how the media's promotion of sexual biases and images affects individual and consumer behavior.

"Shattering the Glass Ceiling" (1999, Insight Media, 30 minutes)

Until recently, only a small percentage of women were in the workforce, and they were restricted to lower-paying positions. This program looks at how more women are shattering the glass ceiling by assuming senior management positions in traditionally male-dominated executive offices.

"Women in American Politics" (1992, Insight Media, 60 minutes)

Highlighting the rising number of women on the American political scene, this video discusses the challenges women candidates face and considers the importance of female participation in politics. It features such politicians as Pat Schroeder, Lynn Martin, and Carol Moseley Braun.

"Women of Vision" (1999, Insight Media, 80 minutes)

Profiling 18 women active in independent feminist film and video, this video examines their work and the range of political and aesthetic viewpoints they express.

"Women in the Workplace" (1998, Insight Media, 20 minutes)

Featuring women of varied ethnic and economic backgrounds and education levels, this video discusses the challenges posed to women as they attempt to build solid career paths. It highlights the importance of education and personal motivation over glamour and body size, and stresses that women can be role models in demonstrating respect, perseverance, independence, and constructive cooperation.

Chapter 14

The Ever-Changing U.S. Mosaic

Chapter 14 At-A-Glance

Detailed Outline	Instructor Resources	Print Supplements	Media Supplements	Professor Notes
Ethnic Consciousness Country of Origin as a Factor	**Lecture Topics:** The ability of new immigrants to keep in contact with their country of origin and the impact it has on acculturation.	**Test Bank** **Textbook Review Questions: #1**	**PowerPoint Media:** "U.S. Immigrants: A Multicultural Journey" (1998, Insight Media, 21 min.) **www.ablongman.com/parrillo**	
The Three-Generation Hypothesis	**Lecture Topic:** Marcus Hansen's "Law of the Return of the Third Generation." Ethnic revival patterns.	**Test Bank**	**PowerPoint Media:** "Hispanic Americans: the Second Generation" (1995, Films for the Humanities & Sciences, 44 min.) **www.ablongman.com/parrillo**	
Recent Immigrants and Adjustment	**Lecture Topics:** Transnationalism, social capital, segmented assimilation, and naturalization.	**Test Bank**	**PowerPoint Media:** American Dream, American Nightmare" (2000, Insight Media, 50 min.) "The Changing Face of America and the World" (2001, Insight Media, 60 min.) **www.ablongman.com/parrillo**	

Ethnicity as a Social Process Symbolic Ethnicity	**Lecture Topics:** The creation of a pluralistic U.S. society.	**Test Bank Textbook Review Questions:** #2	**PowerPoint Media:** "Domino: Interracial People and the Search for Identity" (1994, Films for the Humanities & Sciences, 44 min.) "Matters of Race" (2003, PBS, 240 min.) "Multicultural Understanding" (2000, Insight Media, 55 min.) **www.ablongman.com/parrillo**	
Current Ethnic Issues Immigration Fears Bilingual Education Multiculturalism	**Lecture Topics:** Current trends in minority and majority response patterns - History repeats itself. Anti-immigration laws and the English-Only Movement. **The International Scene:** Multiculturalism in France **Class Activities:** #1 & 2	**Test Bank Textbook Review Questions:** #3 - 5	**Power Point Media:** "Abandoned: The Betrayal of America's Immigrants" (2000, Insight Media, 55 min.) "America's New Immigration Policy" (2001, Insight Media, 27 min.) "English Only in America?" (1995, Insight Media, 25 min.) "The Future is Now: Celebrating Diversity" (1991, Films for the Humanities & Sciences, 26 min.) "Immigration: Who Has Access to the American Dream?" (1997, Films for the Humanities & Sciences, 28 min.) "The Promised Land: Exploring U.S. Immigration Policy" (2004, Insight Media, 45 min.) "You Can't Say That!" (2001, Films for the Humanities & Sciences, 42 min.) **www.ablongman.com/parrillo**	

Racial and Ethnic Diversity in the Future	Lecture Topics:	Test Bank	PowerPoint	
Indicators of Ethnoreligious Change Undocumented Aliens Beyond Tomorrow	Potential worsening of race relations based on increased diversity and multiculturalism. **Class Activities:** #3	**Textbook Review Questions:** #6	**Media:** "Human Contraband: Selling the American Dream" (2001 Films for the Humanities & Sciences, 28 min.) "Voices: Children Speak Out About Diversity" (2001, Insight Media, 5 segments, 10 min. each) "Why Value Diversity?" (1991, Films for the Humanities & Sciences, 26 min.) **www.ablongman.com/ parrillo**	

CHAPTER 14

THE EVER-CHANGING U.S. MOSAIC

LEARNING OBJECTIVES

1. To examine the variables influencing ethnic consciousness or ethnic revivals

2. To discuss ethnicity as a social process that has varying manifestations

3. To discuss current ethnic issues about immigration, illegal aliens, and bilingual education

4. To examine the varying concepts of multiculturalism and political correctness

5. To suggest the possible future of minority relations in the United States

SUMMARY

1. The immigrants' relationship with their country of origin can affect ethnic consciousness. Greater contact, geographical proximity, and stability or social change in the homeland affect sociocultural patterns and lifestyle, as Sengstock's study of a Chaldean community in Detroit indicates.

2. Hansen's three-generation hypothesis offers a general pattern for an ethnic reawakening. Goering suggested that the revival was a regression because of frustration of full assimilation. Abramson argued that the many dimensions of ethnic diversity preclude any macrosocial theory about ethnic consciousness. The interplay of culture and social structure enables or retrains groups to achieve economic success.

3. The white ethnic revival generated many interpretations: a backlash to the civil rights movement; a final stage of assimilation affirming Hansen's hypothesis; a sign of pluralism and unmeltable ethnics; and proof of ethnic resiliency despite assimilation. Gans argues that the resurgence exists only in the minds of a few ethnic academics; it is really a misnomer, he claims, since it reflects a working-class achievement of political power only.

4. Another view is that ethnicity is a continuous variable, not an ascribed attribute with only pluralism and assimilation as discrete categories. Ethnic consciousness can occur and crystallize within work relationships, common residential areas, normal communication, or ethnic organizational participation. Lieberson and Waters noted that links between demographic size and location influence interaction patterns, exogamy, and assimilation. Alba tells of a twilight of ethnicity for those of European ancestry and for them symbolic ethnicity, not day-to-day ethnicity, is the norm. Similarly, African Americans express symbolic ethnicity through clothing and celebration of Kwanzaa.

5. With 5 of every 6 immigrants now from Developing World countries, many native-born Americans both fear and oppose the current influx. Opposition rests on (1) concern about the country's ability to absorb many immigrants, (2) their larger share of population growth given the nation's low birth rate, and (3) worries about their economic impact, although studies show that immigrants have a strong, positive impact.

6. Perhaps 6 million illegal immigrants are now in the United States, about half of them visitors (tourists, students, business) who have overstayed their visas. The Southwest draws most public attention, where Mexicans dominate the list at 74 percent of those apprehended. In 1994, California voters epitomized Americans' hostility, approving California's Proposition 187 to deny public health and education benefits to illegal aliens.

7. Bilingual education only involves 1 in 4 students with limited-English proficiency (LEP). The rest are in ESL classes. The National Education Association (NEA) recommends English and another language for all students (English-plus) Critics charge the programs are too costly, often staffed by paraprofessionals themselves not fluent in English, and that it promotes "ethnic tribalism". Proponents claim it reduces the minority dropout rate and helps students adjust to a new language, new school system, and new society. Recent studies have found bilingual programs successful in aiding limited-English-proficient students, but one study found immersion programs equally fruitful. Other studies find no significant difference in educational achievement and, in 1995, the New York City Board of Education found bilingual programs counterproductive, calling them "prisons."

8. The "English-only movement" is a nativist reaction against foreigners and, by 2001, English-only had passed in 26 states and been rejected in 13 others. Critics charge the movement is derisive and unnecessary. English is *de facto* the nation's official language and studies show almost all Hispanic American parents emphasize mastery of English as very important. Numerous studies show that immigrant parents encourage their children to learn English and that most immigrants in fact do speak English. Still, 73 percent of Americans think English should be made the official language.

9. Multiculturalism began as a movement for inclusion of curriculum material about non-European peoples. Some multiculturalists later rejected a common bond of identity and advocated instead minority nationalism or separatist pluralism. One issue at colleges has been courses in Western civilization. The debate between pluralists and assimilationists is perhaps never ending, since both will always be part of a diverse society.

10. The International Scene box profiles contrasting views in France about diversity, allowing for U.S. comparisons.

11. Political correctness began as a coalition movement to create a tolerant atmosphere on campuses for all peoples. After lobbying for inclusion of courses on racism, sexism, and diversity, the next step became behavior and speech codes. Critics charged politically correct advocates with intolerance, watering down the curriculum, and violating First Amendment rights. A 1992 Supreme Court ruling apparently overturns the speech codes, but in other areas advocates on both sides continue to lock horns.

12. The Census Bureau offers projections for 2050 about the U.S. population composition based on current birth and migration rates. In 1990 the population was 69 percent white, 13 percent black, 13 percent Hispanic, 4 percent Asian, and 1 percent Native American. The 2050 projections are 50 percent white, 24 percent Hispanic, 15 percent black, 8 percent Asian, and 1 percent Native American. These projections, however, may illustrate the Dillingham Flaw, since today's categories may not have the same meaning in the mid-21st century. Hispanics, for example, may intermarry and no longer be distinct.

13. As happened with earlier groups, ethnoreligious changes will likely occur. Interethnic and interracial marriages already taking place are one indicator of the blending of peoples that caution us about predicting future group status. The Catholic American population should grow from one-fourth to one-third of the total because of high immigration from Catholic countries. Similarly, the U.S. Muslim population should grow from 1 to 5 percent.

14. The nation's increasing diversity means continuance of the dual realities of assimilation and pluralism. A greater multiracial society could result in worse race relations or improvement through the deconstruction of rigid racial categories. As the level of education attainment rises, perhaps, so too will greater appreciation and tolerance for others.

CLASS ACTIVITIES

(Each of the following topics lends itself to either small group or class-wide discussion.)

1. The issue of immigration should stimulate some good discussion. How many people should we allow to come here? What impact do they have on the country? How does this third great migration wave compare to the previous two in terms of that impact? What if our family members had been prevented from immigrating?

2. Bilingual education provides another excellent opportunity for extensive discussion. What are the arguments against it? How valid are they? What of the English-only movement? What of the transition approach compared to the maintenance approach? Remind the class that language acquisition has always been a gradual part of the acculturation process, as illustrated by the existence of ethnic subcommunities, the text quotations of Washington and Franklin in Chapter 5, as well as the example of the seventeenth-century Dutch Americans who waited 110 years before introducing English into their schools.

3. What should we do about illegal aliens? Was the amnesty program a mistake? Does it encourage the illegal immigration? Should we seal our borders more effectively? Do the illegal aliens burden our taxpayers or do they help the local economies? These and related questions offer a third opportunity for some vigorous class discussion.

INTERNET RESOURCES

At this book's Web site (http://www.ablongman.com/parrillo), students should select the cover icon, then Chapter 14 to find a variety of links, exercises, and activities pertinent to this content.

MEDIA MATERIALS

"Abandoned: The Betrayal of America's Immigrants" (2000, Insight Media, 55 minutes)

This video depicts the severity of current detention and deportation policies, showing how political asylum seekers wait for years in county jails, while residents are torn from their American families and sent to countries they barely know.

"America's New Immigration Policy" (2001, Insight Media, 27 minutes)

After September 11 arguments for and against immigration have given way to how immigration impacts U.S. security. This program examines these issues and features Mark Krikorian, executive director of the Center for Immigration Studies, and Roy Beck, author of *The Case Against Immigration*.

"American Dream, American Nightmare" (2000, Insight Media, 50 minutes)

Using the true stories of immigrants, this video examines the mistreatment and bureaucratic ineptitude that many non-citizens have experienced in dealing with the INS. It shows how the INS imprisons detainees or jails them for petty crimes and disregards family unity.

"The Changing Face of America and the World" (2001, Insight Media, 60 minutes)

This video explores rapidly changing demographic trends in the United States and around the world. It examines the population changes taking place within the United States and considers the impact of these changes on institutions and communities.

"Domino: Interracial People and the Search for Identity" (1994, Films for the Humanities & Sciences, 44 minutes)

> Explores, through the stories of six interracial people, the issues of racial identity, cultural isolation, and the search for community, ultimately demonstrating how living intimately with two cultures can be a source of strength and enrichment.

"English Only in America?" (1995, Films for the Humanities & Sciences, 25 minutes)

> When California passed a law making English its official language, it set off a storm of legal and social debate that continues to rage today. In this program, advocates for and against the policy examine the topic from social, legal, and educational standpoints.

"The Future is Now: Celebrating Diversity" (1991, Films for the Humanities & Sciences, 26 minutes)

> Shows how to meet the demands of a diverse work force; how schools can help prepare students; how businesses can help build bridges; and how all Americans can and must learn to value, respect, and benefit from diversity in society and in the workplace.

"Hispanic Americans: the Second Generation" (1995, Films for the Humanities & Sciences, 44 minutes)

> Examines how second-generation Hispanics are adapting to U.S. society, maintaining their Latino roots while assimilating into the mainstream. Some famous and everyday Hispanic Americans discuss the role of family and ongoing battles with stereotyping.

"Human Contraband: Selling the American Dream" (2001, Films for the Humanities & Sciences, 28 minutes)

> Investigates the lucrative business of smuggling desperate people from all over the world through Mexico into the United States. Ted Koppel interviews INS official on multilateral efforts to combat steady flow of illegal entries.

"Immigration: Who Has Access to the American Dream?" (1997, Films for the Humanities & Sciences, 28 minutes)

> What should be our immigration policy? How many should we let in? Should anyone receive preferential treatment? What about illegal immigration? This program examines those issues through the immigrants' eyes and the organizations assisting them.

"Matters of Race" (2003, PBS, 240 minutes)

> This PBS program examines race and its role in American democracy in the face of today's rapidly changing multiracial and multicultural society. It probes the identity of small-town America and explores the polarities of race and ethnic communities.

"Multicultural Understanding" (2001, Insight Media, 20 minutes)

> American culture is unique because it is the creation of a diverse population. Showing how a more diverse culture is a richer culture, this program addresses the erroneousness of imagining that any ethnic, racial, or religious group could be superior to another.

"The Promised Land: Exploring U.S. Immigration Policy" (2004, Insight Media, 45 minutes)

> This program, narrated by Tom Brokaw, addresses contentious issues in U.S. immigration policy through the dramatic store of The Golden Venture, a Chinese ship that ran aground near the Statue of Liberty. The incident resulted in hundreds of Chinese swimming for American shores in an effort to become citizens. The program examines how to strike a balance between offering political asylum to those who need it and protecting the integrity of American borders.

"U.S. Immigrants: A Multicultural Journey" (1998, Insight Media, 21 minutes)

> Offers an historical look at immigration into the United States over the millennia. It looks at the emotional and economic forces that brought people to this continent and speculates on the future of immigration in the United States.

"Voices: Children Speak Out About Diversity" (2001, Insight Media, 5 segments, 10 minutes each)

> The richness of the United States lies in its wealth of differences. Why then is this unique human richness also a source of division and despair? This set features teens from across the United States exploring the diversity dilemma with candor and passion.

"Why Value Diversity?" (1991, Films for the Humanities & Sciences, 26 minutes)

> Looks at the realities of a multiracial, multilingual work force in a society where racism and sexism still exist. An attorney, a corporate executive, a human resources manager and teacher explain steps individuals can take to benefit from the new realities.

"You Can't Say That!" (2001, Films for the Humanities & Sciences, 42 minutes)

An ABC news program explores growing constraints on free speech made in the interest of protecting the public from offense. Considers the paranoia in academic, political, and business sectors that has led to the creation of virtual "speech police."

TEST BANK

Chapter 1   The Study of Minorities

Multiple Choice Questions

1) Aristotle said, "We like those who resemble us, and are engaged in the same pursuits." Which of the following concepts best represents Aristotle's statement?

    A) similarity and attraction

    B) identical preferences

    C) opposites attract

    D) group identification preference

    E) none of the above

Answer: A
Page Ref: 4

2) Social distance studies have found

    A) an erratic pattern, depending on world or economic situations.

    B) a fairly consistent pattern over the decades.

    C) greater distance only between racial groups.

    D) elimination of social distance between groups after two generations.

Answer: B
Page Ref: 5

3) Natives usually perceive strangers

    A) objectively.   B) hospitably.   C) categorically.   D) indifferently.

Answer: C
Page Ref: 8

4) Which of the following categories of people are most tolerant of each other?

    A) young   B) well educated

    C) upper income   D) all of the above

Answer: D
Page Ref: 8

5) In a new social setting, strangers

    A) experience every situation as potentially problematic.

    B) lack the natives' knowledge of shared realities.

    C) are acutely aware of things unnoticed by the natives.

    D) all of the above

Answer: D
Page Ref: 9

6) According to Parillo, sociology is

    A) just like psychology.

    B) study of human relationships.

    C) study of patterns of behavior.

    D) study of individuals.

    E) both B and C.

Answer: E
Page Ref: 10

7) Functional theory does <u>not</u> emphasize

    A) social equilibrium.   B) interdependent societal parts.

    C) imbalance of power.   D) adjustments to restore societal stability.

Answer: C
Page Ref: 11

8) A 2001 study showed that more than 50 percent of newlyweds met their spouses in the workplace. Sociologically, meeting a spouse at work would be considered a

    A) latent function of workplaces.   B) manifest function of workplaces.

    C) latent dysfunction of workplaces.   D) a manifest dysfunction of workplaces.

Answer: A
Page Ref: 11

9) Karl Marx believed that the elite exploited the masses and that this exploitation created tensions and disagreements. Marx's theory is best known as

    A) conflict perspective.   B) functionalist perspective.

    C) interactionist perspective.   D) unfair perspective.

Answer: A
Page Ref: 12

10) Pursuing the question of "Who benefits?" from a particular situation suggests which likely perspective?

    A) functionalist   B) conflict   C) interactionist   D) societist

Answer: B
Page Ref: 12

11) A sociologist who investigates how people interpret the situations they are in is probably a(n)

    A) functionalist.   B) conflict theorist.

    C) interactionist.   D) societist.

Answer: C
Page Ref: 13

12) A minority group is

    A) numerically smaller than the dominant group.

    B) less powerful than the dominant group.

    C) more powerful than the dominant group.

    D) both A and C.

Answer: B
Page Ref: 14

13) When marrying, members of a minority group usually practice

    A) endogamy.

    B) exogamy.

    C) polyandry.

    D) polygamy.

    E) all of the above

Answer: A
Page Ref: 16

14) An example of an ascribed status is a

    A) writer.   B) Mormon convert.

    C) female.   D) new immigrant.

Answer: C
Page Ref: 16

15) According to Parillo, a category of people who share visible biological characteristics and are regarded as a single group is a(n)

    A) race.   B) ethnic group.   C) social deviant.   D) status.

Answer: A
Page Ref: 17

16) Ethnicity is

    A) another term for "race."

    B) a false and arbitrary classification of people.

    C) a term used to refer to European peoples.

    D) learned or acquired cultural traits shared by a people.

Answer: D
Page Ref: 18

17) Which of the following is an ethnic group?

    A) Native Americans   B) Asian Americans

    C) Black Americans   D) Bulgarian Americans

Answer: D
Page Ref: 18

18) Susan, a Texas cattle rancher, thinks the Japanese custom of eating raw fish is disgusting. This is an example of

    A) ethnicity.   B) ethnocentrism.

    C) poor taste.   D) cultural relativism.

Answer: B
Page Ref: 18

19) Juan believes that hispanic families are superior to white families. This belief is an example of which theory?

    A) Social-referent group theory   B) Ethnic preference theory

    C) Social-identity theory   D) Outgroup discrimination theory

Answer: C
Page Ref: 19

20) By ingroup, sociologists mean

    A) group immigrating into the country.

    B) the dominant group.

    C) the group to which an individual belongs and feels loyalty.

    D) the reference group others imitate.

Answer: C
Page Ref: 18

21) In American culture, such things as freedom, individualism and equal opportunity are deemed to be highly desirable. In sociological terms these concepts are

    A) mores.   B) desires.   C) norms.   D) values.   E) folkways.

Answer: D
Page Ref: 23

22) Social identity theory helps explain

    A) upward mobility.   B) ethnic antagonism.

    C) ingroup favoritism.   D) immigration quotas.

Answer: C
Page Ref: 19

23) Underrepresenting non–European material exemplifies

    A) Afrocentrism.   B) Eurocentrism.

    C) categoric knowing.   D) reciprocal typification.

Answer: B
Page Ref: 22

24) Arguing Western civilization derives from the black African influence on Egyptian civilization is a bolder form of

    A) Afrocentrism.   B) categoric knowing.

    C) false consciousness.   D) interactionist theory.

Answer: A
Page Ref: 22

25) Pluralist advocates criticize which of the following?

    A) Afrocentrism   B) ethnocentrism

    C) Eurocentrism   D) all of the above

Answer: D
Page Ref: 23

26) The main focus or unit of analysis for sociologists is

A) the group.

B) the individual.

C) the stranger.

D) none of the above.

Answer: A
Page Ref: 25

27) Studying race and ethnic relations is

A) easier than most other subjects because of our familiarity with minority problems.

B) easier because most people are sensitive to the problems and needs of others.

C) difficult because our values, attitudes, and experiences make our objectivity almost impossible.

D) difficult because the subject defies a logical or scientific explanation.

Answer: C
Page Ref: 23

28) Which of the following illustrates the Dillingham Flaw?

A) emphasis on preserving one's culture

B) distrust of political solutions to end discrimination

C) criticism of an immigrant group, compared to an earlier one

D) assumption that a minority group is lazy or immoral

Answer: C
Page Ref: 24

29) An ethnic group held up as a role model in contrast to a newly arrived group was probably

A) once an object of scorn and condemnation itself.

B) the beneficiary of governmental assistance.

C) large in numbers to deter criticism about their immigration.

D) quick to learn English and assimilate.

Answer: A
Page Ref: 24

30) Mills states that an issue is a public matter when it is

A) not relevant to group behavior study in sociology.

B) less important than the welfare of the group.

C) only important to sociologists after thorough study of the group.

D) intricately connected to the larger historical context of society.

Answer: D
Page Ref: 25

True/False Questions

1) Many people still call the United States a great melting pot where people of all races, religions, and nationalities come to be free and to improve their lives.

Answer: TRUE
Page Ref: 3

2) Within any society, groupings of people by race, religion, tribe, culture, or lifestyle can generate a sense of familiarity and belonging.

Answer: FALSE
Page Ref: 4

3) According to Aristotle, "We like those who resemble us, and are engaged in the same pursuits."

Answer: TRUE
Page Ref: 4

4) Social distance refers to how far away your relatives and friends live.

Answer: FALSE
Page Ref: 5

5) Natives tend to perceive strangers in an abstract, typified way.

Answer: TRUE
Page Ref: 8

6) Sociologist use historical documents, reports, surveys, ethnographies and direct observation to systematically gather empirical evidence about intergroup relations.

Answer: TRUE
Page Ref: 10

7) Manifest functions are better than latent functions.

Answer: FALSE
Page Ref: 11

8) Conflict theorist ask the important question, "Who benefits?"

Answer: TRUE
Page Ref: 12

9) Interactionists focus on the macrosocial world of personal interaction patterns in everyday life.

Answer: FALSE
Page Ref: 15

10) Functionalists believe that society is a stable, cooperative social system in which everything has a function and provides the basis of a harmonious society.

Answer: TRUE
Page Ref: 15

Essay Questions

1) Discuss how perceptions of strangers affect interactions.
Page Ref: 8

2) Explain the primary changes in social distance results from 1977 and 2001.
Page Ref: 7

3) Compare and contrast Simmel and Schutz's view of the role of a stranger.
Page Ref: 8–9

4) Compare and contrast the three major sociological perspectives in studying minorities.
Page Ref: 15

5) Explain the importance of objectivity in the scientific study of sociology.
Page Ref: 23

6) Explain the differences between racial and ethnic groups.
Page Ref: 17–18

7) Discuss and illustrate ethnocentrism as a universal human condition.
Page Ref: 18

8) Discuss the value of utilizing the concepts of ingroup and outgroup in the study of majority and minority groups.
Page Ref: 18–19

9) Compare and contrast the three main sociological perspectives.
Page Ref: 15

10) Explain the Dillingham Flaw and how it affects judgment about today's immigrants.
Page Ref: 24

Chapter 2 Culture and Social Structure

Multiple Choice Questions

1) Which of the following is a characteristic of culture?

    A) It is shared.

    B) It is acquired.

    C) It is transmitted from one generation to the next.

    D) all of the above

Answer: D
Page Ref: 33–34

2) The primary transmitter of our culture is

    A) the schools.   B) everyday experience.

    C) language.   D) facial expressions.

Answer: C
Page Ref: 33

3) According to interactionists, social interaction among people of different cultures may be difficult because

    A) the two parties do not share the same definitions of symbols.

    B) people have a natural reluctance to relate to strangers.

    C) strangers are intimidated by the natives of the host country.

    D) one group tries to dominate the other.

Answer: A
Page Ref: 34–35

4) The Thomas Theorem states that

    A) you've got to be taught to hate and fear.

    B) if people define a situation as real, it becomes real in its consequences.

    C) the world of reality is taken for granted.

    D) each generation passes its cultural values on to the next generation.

Answer: B
Page Ref: 35

5) Which of the following is an example of material culture?

    A) money

    B) the exchange of ideas

    C) religion

    D) acculturation

    E) none of the above

Answer: A
Page Ref: 31–32

6) The fact that cultures owe a substantial debt to other cultures because of the spread of ideas, inventions, and practices is called

    A) cultural transmission.

    B) convergence.

    C) cross–cultural impregnation.

    D) cultural diffusion.

    E) Both B and C are correct.

Answer: D
Page Ref: 37

7) Students who sit quietly in class and take careful notes are fulfilling societal expectations of behavior, which are called

    A) mores.   B) values.

    C) norms.   D) material culture.

Answer: C
Page Ref: 32

8) Settling in an area already containing family, friends, or compatriots is known as

    A) chain migration.   B) joined resettlement.

    C) parallel social institutions.   D) recycling.

Answer: A
Page Ref: 39

9) Sociologists call a minority group's establishment of its own clubs, organizations, stores, churches, newspapers, and schools

    A) duplication.   B) parallel social institutions.

    C) redundant social patterns.   D) subcultural networking.

Answer: B
Page Ref: 39

10) In convergent subcultures we tend to see

    A) continued residential clustering.

    B) everyday ethnicity in language, dress, and cultural behavior.

    C) a gradual assimilation process.

    D) all of the above.

Answer: C
Page Ref: 43

11) Which group illustrates a persistent subculture?

    A) Amish   B) Irish   C) Germans   D) Italians

Answer: A
Page Ref: 40

12) Dominique whistled at her brother to get his attention. This is an example of using

    A) paralinguistic signals.   B) language.

    C) vocal communication.   D) nonverbal notation.

Answer: A
Page Ref: 35

13) Technological improvements in communication and transportation

    A) have no real impact upon dominant–minority relations.

    B) may actually encourage pluralism in the host country.

    C) accelerate the assimilation process because they make for a smaller world.

    D) are important only because they encourage more people from distant places to migrate to the U.S.

Answer: B
Page Ref: 37

14) When Juan arrived in Milan he was surprised to find that people drank wine during working lunches. This is an example of

    A) cultural transmission.   B) culture irrelevance.

    C) culture diffusion.   D) culture shock.

Answer: D
Page Ref: 38

15) The culture of poverty refers to

   A) poor peoples' contributions to U.S. culture in folk music, literary subjects, and folklore.

   B) cultural traits of the poor transmitted from one generation to the next, creating a perpetual underclass.

   C) the cultural tastes of the poor.

   D) blacks only; other minority groups do not fit this framework.

Answer: B
Page Ref: 45

16) Relationships between majority and minority groups are influenced by differences in culture, as well as

   A) structural conditions.   B) acculturation.

   C) cultural ethnocentrism.   D) None of the above are true.

Answer: A
Page Ref: 42

17) Sal is an undergraduate, a member of the Dean's List and a pizza parlor manager. These are all examples of a(n)

   A) achieved status.   B) ascribed status.

   C) achieved norms.   D) college life.

Answer: B
Page Ref: 42

18) The reputational method involves

   A) asking people how they thought others compared to them.

   B) asking people for references.

   C) beliefs about how your coworkers feel about you.

   D) asking someone to tell you how they feel about you.

Answer: A
Page Ref: 43

19) Warner's Yankee City study found an important link between social class status and

   A) length of residence in the U.S.

   B) size of the immigrant population in the community.

   C) nearness of one's homeland.

   D) all of the above.

Answer: D
Page Ref: 43

20) One connection between ethnicity and social class, according to Leggett, is

   A) the lower the ethnic status, the higher the level of class consciousness.

   B) the lower the ethnic status, the lower the level of class consciousness.

   C) working-class ethnics are less hostile to other minorities than middle-class natives.

   D) ethnic antagonism occurs mostly within social-class groupings rather than across social class lines.

Answer: A
Page Ref: 44

21) Moynihan believed that the explanation for high unemployment, welfare dependency and other social problems was

   A) poor social class skills.   B) pluralism.

   C) family deterioration.   D) culture shock.

Answer: C
Page Ref: 45

22) Milton Gordon's ethclass groupings represent

   A) the eventual decline of ethnicity as a significant factor.

   B) the supremacy of ethnicity over social class because of ethnic reawakening.

   C) the subsocieties resulting from the intersection of ethnicity and social class.

   D) an abstract concept, not one of primary relationships.

Answer: C
Page Ref: 45

23) Rodman's belief that all people share the same values of a society, but that the lower class adopt additional more realistic values is known as

   A) value-driven belief.   B) cultural extension.

   C) lower class degeneration.   D) value-stretch approach.

Answer: D
Page Ref: 48

24) Park's theory of a race relations cycle suggested

   A) economics drive the variance in intergroup relations.

   B) an inevitable and irreversible process toward assimilation.

   C) little assimilation because of racial differences.

   D) racial problems only exist in the western world.

Answer: B
Page Ref: 57

25) The equation A+B+C=A illustrates which concept?

    A) amalgamation   B) assimilation   C) desegregation   D) pluralism

Answer: B
Page Ref: 57

26) Cultural differentiation refers to

    A) the differences that are present between two cultures.

    B) the likelihood of similarity between two groups.

    C) pluralism.

    D) assimilation.

Answer: A
Page Ref: 50

27) The equation A+B+C=D illustrates which concept?

    A) amalgamation   B) assimilation   C) immigration   D) pluralism

Answer: A
Page Ref: 59

28) Cynthia began working in the copy room of a large corporation but is now the manager of an entire corporate division. This is an example of

    A) occupational mobility.   B) luck.

    C) right place phenomenon.   D) career achieved status.

Answer: A
Page Ref: 52

29) Ralf Dahrendorf sees a correlation between a group's economic position and the

    A) intensity of the assimilation process.

    B) intensity of its conflict with the dominant society.

    C) intensity of segregation.

    D) intensity of the pluralism process.

Answer: B
Page Ref: 64

30) Pluralism

    A) hampers societal harmony because it promotes differences among groups.

    B) has been a fact throughout the nation's history.

    C) has only recently existed because of a growing ethnic and racial consciousness.

    D) is a temporary social phenomenon until assimilation inevitably occurs.

Answer: B
Page Ref: 63

True/False Questions

1) Nonmaterial culture changes faster than material culture.

Answer: FALSE
Page Ref: 31

2) Most minority groups eventually adapt their distinctive cultural traits to those of the host society.

Answer: TRUE
Page Ref: 33

3) Racism and group superiority themes are part of the United States core value orientations.

Answer: TRUE
Page Ref: 32

4) Linguistic relativity of language means that every race has its own language.

Answer: FALSE
Page Ref: 34

5) Paralinguistic signals include sounds but not words.

Answer: TRUE
Page Ref: 35

6) Ralph Linton calculated that any given culture contains about 90 percent borrowed elements.

Answer: TRUE
Page Ref: 37

7) Convergent subcultures come together to create a brand new culture.

Answer: FALSE
Page Ref: 40

8) An ascribed status is one that someone has given to us as a gift.

Answer: FALSE
Page Ref: 42

9) In his book, The Ethnic Myth, Stephen Steinberg stressed the importance of social structure and minimized cultural factors.

Answer: TRUE
Page Ref: 44

10) The lower class rejects the less attainable values of the majority society and adopts a value-stretch approach instead.

Answer: FALSE
Page Ref: 48

Essay Questions

1) Explain the difference between material and nonmaterial culture. Which would change faster?
Page Ref: 31

2) Explain how knowledge of language and cultural symbols shape our perception of reality.
Page Ref: 33-34

3) Explain and illustrate the differences between cultural diffusion and cultural transmission.
Page Ref: 37-38

4) Discuss Robin Williams' 15 common core value orientations and the impact they've had on U.S. culture.
Page Ref: 32

5) Discuss both sides of the culture-of-poverty controversy. What position do most sociologists take?
Page Ref: 45-47

6) Discuss the interrelationships between ethnicity and social class.
Page Ref: 44

7) Discuss the concept of assimilation, amalgamation and pluralism.
Page Ref: 56-64

8) Compare and contrast Stephen Steinberg and Thomas Sowell's views of a minority group's economic success.
Page Ref: 44-45

9) Explain the four stages of Robert E. Park's race-relations cycle. Give an example to help illustrate.
Page Ref: 49–50

10) Compare and contrast paternalism and competitive systems.
Page Ref: 52–53

Chapter 3 Prejudice and Discrimination

Multiple Choice Questions

1) Prejudice exists at which of the following levels?

    A) cognitive   B) emotional

    C) action   D) all of the above

Answer: D
Page Ref: 70-71

2) George is trying to understand prejudice. His professor tells him to consider which of the following?

    A) Prejudice may be the result of frustration

    B) Prejudice exists on three levels.

    C) Prejudice may be either positive or negative.

    D) All of the above are true.

Answer: D
Page Ref: 71

3) When a person holds generalized beliefs and perceptions about a group, prejudice exists at which level?

    A) cognitive   B) emotional

    C) action-orientation   D) none of the above

Answer: A
Page Ref: 70

4) If a minority group arouses feelings in an individual, prejudice exists at which level?

    A) cognitive   B) emotional

    C) action-orientation   D) all of the above

Answer: B
Page Ref: 71

5) If a person behaves in ways that maintain the inequality between two groups, prejudice exists at which level?

    A) cognitive   B) emotional

    C) action-orientation   D) none of the above

Answer: C
Page Ref: 71

6) Denigrating another group to justify our maltreatment of them is called

   A) cognitive development.   B) self–justification.

   C) scapegoating.   D) socialization.

   Answer: B
   Page Ref: 71

7) Harry meets the criteria for Adorno's authoritarian personality, therefore he is probably

   A) the recipient of a harsh upbringing.

   B) lower class.

   C) not well educated.

   D) intolerant of weakness.

   E) all of the above.

   Answer: E
   Page Ref: 72

8) Lacking the same standard of living compared to most members of society is called

   A) absolute deprivation.   B) poverty.

   C) relative deprivation.   D) value–deficiency.

   Answer: C
   Page Ref: 74

9) Juanita likes to blame her little brother for her failure to do her chores but her brother was not even home. Juanita is clearly engaging in

   A) self–justification.   B) subjugation.

   C) scapegoating.   D) escapism.

   Answer: C
   Page Ref: 74

10) Which of the following statement is true?

   A) The higher the social class, the lower the authoritarianism.

   B) The lower the social class, the higher the authoritarianism.

   C) The higher the level of education the higher the authoritarianism.

   D) The lower the level of education the higher the authoritarianism.

   E) Both A and D are true

   Answer: E
   Page Ref: 73

11) The process by which we learn and internalize prejudicial attitudes about others is called

    A) cognitive development.   B) self–justification.

    C) scapegoating.   D) socialization.

Answer: D
Page Ref: 76

12) An excellent example of economic competition breeding conflict is that of the

    A) Chinese.   B) Quakers.   C) Mormons.   D) Norwegians

Answer: A
Page Ref: 76

13) Talcott Parsons developed a concept that linked the psychological and sociological aspects of frustration–aggression called

    A) prejudice.   B) free floating.

    C) permanent anger.   D) cultural irritation.

Answer: B
Page Ref: 75

14) Which of the following best explains the cause of prejudice?

    A) There appears to be no single cause of prejudice.

    B) Prejudice is a normal human attribute.

    C) Prejudice is an outgrowth of discrimination.

    D) All prejudice is based upon economic factors.

Answer: A
Page Ref: 70–75

15) Which of the following is <u>not</u> a characteristic of a stereotype?

    A) oversimplified generalization

    B) emphasizes variance from societal norms

    C) recognizes individual differences

    D) once established, difficult to eradicate

Answer: C
Page Ref: 78–80

16) An ethnophaulism is a

    A) visible ethnic community.

    B) derogatory word or expression to describe a group.

    C) biased condition for or against a particular group.

    D) term to describe ethnic self-awareness and/or embarrassment.

Answer: B
Page Ref: 80

17) Studies of stereotyped beliefs among three generations of college undergraduates showed

    A) substantial changes.

    B) college students do not stereotype others.

    C) their elimination.

    D) their persistence.

Answer: D
Page Ref: 75

18) An ethnic group member might tell an ethnic joke about themselves to an outgroup member in order to

    A) undermine the stereotype by ridiculing it.

    B) dissociate oneself from stereotypes of one's group.

    C) maintain the imbalance of power.

    D) reaffirm negative self-image.

Answer: A
Page Ref: 80–81

19) Studies of television programming reveal

    A) major success in eradicating stereotyped images.

    B) perpetuation of racial and sexual stereotypes.

    C) more women shown as independent role models.

    D) Asians increasingly portrayed doing interesting things.

Answer: B
Page Ref: 82

20) Studies measuring the impact of television on children's attitudes indicate

    A) no correlation at all.

    B) inconclusive findings.

    C) significant correlations.

    D) black, not white, children are more easily influenced.

Answer: C
Page Ref: 82

21) Stereotypes

    A) are predominantly true.

    B) deny individuals the right to be judged and treated on the basis of their own personal merit.

    C) are always hurtful and negative.

    D) none of the above.

Answer: B
Page Ref: 79

22) Aronson and Osherow's experiments on the jigsaw method

    A) had no effect on prejudice reduction.

    B) wreaked special hardship on minority children.

    C) lowered self-esteem among minority children.

    D) enhanced peer liking and successfully taught content.

Answer: D
Page Ref: 86

23) Inconsistency in education reducing prejudice results from

    A) selective perception of information.

    B) contrast between classroom and real-life situations.

    C) inadequate information for teaching about intergroup relations.

    D) both A and B

Answer: D
Page Ref: 87

24) According to Robert Merton, discrimination against a particular group is

    A) always the acting-out of prejudice.   B) only practiced by prejudiced people

    C) not always the result of prejudice.   D) both A and B

Answer: C
Page Ref: 90

25) An employer who strongly dislikes a racial group hires them anyway because of legal and social pressures, typifying the

    A) unprejudiced nondiscriminator.   B) unprejudiced discriminator.

    C) prejudiced nondiscriminator.   D) prejudiced discriminator.

Answer: C
Page Ref: 91

26) Alfred had no prejudices towards Blacks but when his friends make derogatory comments to Black kids he does nothing to stop them. Alfred is a(n)

    A) unprejudiced nondiscriminator.   B) unprejudiced discriminator.

    C) prejudiced nondiscriminator.   D) prejudiced discriminator.

Answer: B
Page Ref: 90

27) Affirmative action originated with an executive order by President

    A) Franklin D. Roosevelt.   B) John F. Kennedy.

    C) Richard M. Nixon.   D) Ronald Reagan.

Answer: A
Page Ref: 93

28) The Bakke decision

    A) eliminated racial quotas in all fields.

    B) reaffirmed racial quotas in all fields.

    C) reaffirmed race, but not quotas, as a factor in college admissions.

    D) narrowly applied only to the specifics of the Bakke case.

Answer: C
Page Ref: 94

29) Evidence about the success of affirmative action programs

    A) is clearly positive.   B) is clearly negative.

    C) is mixed.   D) has not yet been found.

Answer: C
Page Ref: 96

30) Racial profiling is

    A) rare.   B) prejudiced.

    C) legally enforced.   D) none of the above.

Answer: B
Page Ref: 97

True/False Questions

1) Ralph Rosudice expanded the definition of prejudice to include "any unreasonable attitude that is unusually resistant to rational influence."

Answer: TRUE
Page Ref: 69

2) Psychological and sociological perspectives complement each other in providing a fuller explanation about intergroup relations.

Answer: TRUE
Page Ref: 70

3) The emotional level of prejudice encompasses the feelings that a majority group arouses in the minority group.

Answer: FALSE
Page Ref: 71

4) Self–justification involves denigrating a person or group to justify maltreatment of them.

Answer: TRUE
Page Ref: 71

5) When children are treated harshly they may grow up and displace their aggression on those who are less powerful.

Answer: TRUE
Page Ref: 73

6) Galinsky and Ku (2004) found that those with high self–esteem evaluated an outgroup less positively than those with low self–esteem.

Answer: FALSE
Page Ref: 74

7) Jim Crow laws established segregated public facilities throughout the South.

Answer: TRUE
Page Ref: 76

8) Muzafer Sherif found that intergroup competition at a boys' camp led to a reduction in conflict and hostility.

Answer: FALSE
Page Ref: 77

9) Stereotypes can be positive or negative.

Answer: TRUE
Page Ref: 78

10) An ethnophaulism is a derogatory word or expression used to describe a racial or ethnic group.

Answer: TRUE
Page Ref: 80

Essay Questions

1) Compare and contrast the psychological and sociological analyses of prejudice.
Page Ref: 70

2) Discuss stereotypes, their persistence, and their impact upon intergroup relations.
Page Ref: 78–79

3) Howard J. Ehrlich divides ethnophaulisms into three types. Define ethnophaulisms and explain his three types.
Page Ref: 80

4) What's wrong with ethnic jokes? What's good about them? Explain your answer.
Page Ref: 81–82

5) Discuss the importance of television in helping or hindering intergroup relations.
Page Ref: 82–83

6) Explain the strengths and weaknesses of self–justification as it relates to prejudice.
Page Ref: 71–72

7) Can we reduce prejudice through increased interaction and education? Explain your answer.
Page Ref: 85–86

8) Define discrimination, explaining and illustrating its several levels.
Page Ref: 89–91

9) Using Merton's fourfold typology, explain the interrelationships between prejudice and discrimination.
Page Ref: 90

10) Discuss both sides of the philosophical and realistic issues in the affirmative–action controversy.
Page Ref: 92–93

Chapter 4 Dominant–Minority Relations

Multiple Choice Questions

1) Which factor promotes ethnic group identity?

   A) ethnic–minority media

   B) cohesive community

   C) religion

   D) socialization

   E) all of the above

   Answer: E
   Page Ref: 102

2) Non-Europeans typically develop a(n)

   A) racial–group identity.   B) racial majority.

   C) intergroup bonding.   D) all of the above.

   Answer: A
   Page Ref: 103

3) Which affects responses to prejudice and discrimination?

   A) personality characteristics   B) external factors

   C) social interpretation   D) all of the above

   Answer: D
   Page Ref: 101

4) People of color typically affirm their identity and heritage by

   A) combating their stereotypes.

   B) teaching the younger generation about their racial history.

   C) adopting slogans.

   D) all of the above.

   Answer: D
   Page Ref: 103

5) Deviance among minority-group members is

   A) usually widespread.

   B) usually due to their behavioral characteristics.

   C) often due to poverty and lack of opportunity.

   D) more often due to racial, not ethnic, differences.

Answer: C
Page Ref: 105

6) Which of the following is <u>not</u> an example of deviance?

   A) crime   B) drunkenness

   C) sit-in demonstration   D) vandalism

Answer: C
Page Ref: 106

7) A common reason for defiance as a minority response is

   A) the elimination of discrimination.   B) the overthrow of the government.

   C) drunkenness.   D) juvenile delinquency.

Answer: A
Page Ref: 106

8) Defiant actions are

   A) violent.

   B) peaceful.

   C) illegal.

   D) either peaceful or violent.

   E) none of the above.

Answer: D
Page Ref: 106

9) Accepting a subordinate position in society may result from

   A) social conditioning.

   B) subtle rationalizations.

   C) economic necessity.

   D) desire for personal security.

   E) all of the above.

Answer: E
Page Ref: 107

10) Acceptance maintains the superior position of the dominant group, the subordinate position of the minority group and

A) diminishes conflict between the two groups.

B) the attention of law enforcement.

C) makes everyday life more difficult.

D) none of the above.

Answer: A
Page Ref: 107

11) Minority group status has been improved through all of the following EXCEPT

A) legislation.	B) court decisions.
C) social services.	D) deviance.

Answer: D
Page Ref: 107

12) Living, working, and relaxing within the ethnic community illustrates

A) acceptance. B) avoidance. C) defiance. D) deviance.

Answer: B
Page Ref: 103

13) Deliberately breaking a discriminatory law illustrates

A) acceptance. B) avoidance. C) defiance. D) deviance.

Answer: C
Page Ref: 106

14) Shaniqua has a negative self-image because she is a member of a minority group. As a result, which of the following actions is she most likely to take?

A) She tries to dress like the dominant group and blend in.

B) She tries to start fights with the dominant group.

C) She challenges laws that discriminate against her minority group.

D) none of the above

Answer: A
Page Ref: 108

15) Another term for cumulative causation is

A) marginality.	B) negative self-image.
C) paternalism.	D) vicious circle.

Answer: D
Page Ref: 108–109

16) Calling Jews "clannish" when they went to their own resorts after being denied access to public resorts illustrates

    A) marginality.

    B) negative self-image.

    C) paternalism.

    D) vicious circle.

    E) none of the above.

Answer: D
Page Ref: 109

17) When minorities move out of their neighborhood but still feel outside the societal mainstream, this is an example of

    A) avoidance.   B) marginality.

    C) negative self-image.   D) vicious circle.

Answer: B
Page Ref: 109

18) Tommy has made progress toward fitting in with the dominant group but he hasn't completely broken away from his minority group. More likely than not Tommy is bound to feel

    A) silly.   B) accepted.   C) marginalized.   D) committed.

Answer: C
Page Ref: 109

19) Many Korean Americans own and operate grocery stores in the nation's major cities, typifying the concept of

    A) gentrification.   B) marginality.

    C) middleman minorities.   D) social segregation.

Answer: C
Page Ref: 111

20) Middleman minorities are

    A) members of a racial group other than the dominant group.

    B) permanently stationed in that role.

    C) temporarily stationed in that role.

    D) either B or C.

Answer: D
Page Ref: 111

21) Which is <u>not</u> a legislative effort to control a minority?

    A) immigration quota laws   B) Jim Crow laws

    C) civil rights legislation   D) poll taxes

Answer: C
Page Ref: 112

22) Chinatown would be an example of

    A) spacial segregation.   B) social segregation.

    C) language segregation.   D) all of the above.

Answer: A
Page Ref: 113

23) Preventing others from participating in social, fraternal, service, and other types of activities is known as _____ segregation.

    A) spatial   B) social   C) de jure   D) de facto

Answer: B
Page Ref: 113

24) Expulsion

    A) is an effort to remove a problem rather than resolve it.

    B) has never been practiced in the U.S.

    C) has not occurred since the nineteenth century.

    D) all of the above

Answer: A
Page Ref: 114

25) Julie is afraid of all Middle Easterners ever since 9/11. This is an example of

    A) expulsion.   B) xenophobia.

    C) immigrant anarchy.   D) politicoeconomic independence.

Answer: B
Page Ref: 114

26) Annihilation

    A) has often been practiced in both ancient and modern times.

    B) is sometimes unintended but happens nonetheless.

    C) by definition must be a deliberate and systematic action.

    D) both A and B

Answer: D
Page Ref: 115

27) The increase of hate groups in the 1990s is partly due to

    A) a weakened U.S. economy.   B) public funding.

    C) Internet propaganda.   D) none of the above.

Answer: C
Page Ref: 117

28) The Intelligence Project identifies which of the following as a hate group?

    A) black separatists   B) Christian Identity

    C) Nation of Islam   D) all of the above

Answer: D
Page Ref: 118

29) The greatest number of U.S. hate crimes result from _____ bias.

    A) ethnic   B) racial

    C) religious   D) sexual–orientation

Answer: B
Page Ref: 120

30) By a split labor market, Bonacich means

    A) both agricultural and industrial jobs are available.

    B) equally priced workers compete for limited jobs.

    C) wage differences among workers create problems.

    D) rapid industrial growth splits the job market wide open.

Answer: C
Page Ref: 144

True/False Questions

1) Any group unable to participate fully in the societal mainstream typically develops its own group identity.

Answer: TRUE
Page Ref: 101–102

2) Everyday ethnicity eventually yields to assimilation over the generations.

Answer: TRUE
Page Ref: 102

3) For some minority groups, seeking shelter from prejudice is probably a secondary motivation, following a primary desire to live among their own kind.

Answer: TRUE
Page Ref: 103

4) Deviant behavior among minority groups occurs because of race or ethnicity.

Answer: FALSE
Page Ref: 105

5) Schooling leads to more educationally committed adolescents, the greater their commitment, the lower the rates of delinquency, and vice versa.

Answer: TRUE
Page Ref: 106

6) Defiance is violent and spontaneous.

Answer: FALSE
Page Ref: 106

7) Acceptance as a minority response is less common in the United states than it once was.

Answer: TRUE
Page Ref: 107

8) According to Robert E. Park, a marginal person is on "whom fate has shined upon."

Answer: FALSE
Page Ref: 109

9) Members of a dominant group may react to minority peoples with hostility, indifference, welcoming tolerance, or condescension.

Answer: TRUE
Page Ref: 111

10) Segregation, whether spatial or social, may be voluntary or involuntary.

Answer: TRUE
Page Ref: 113

Essay Questions

1) Discuss the concept of group identity and its positive or negative consequences.
Page Ref: 102

2) Compare and contrast the various response patterns that minorities could follow.
Page Ref: 101–110

3) Discuss how the subjective nature of the criminal justice system impacts on minority groups.
Page Ref: 105

4) Explain four of the factors that might determine the duration of an ethnic-group identity.
Page Ref: 102

5) Explain Gunnar Myrdal's cumulative causation or vicious circle hypothesis.
Page Ref: 108-109

6) What did Robert E. Park's mean when he said that a marginalized person is someone "whom fate has condemned to live in two societies and in two not merely different but antagonistic cultures"?
Page Ref: 109

7) Explain what is meant by middleman minorities and give an example.
Page Ref: 111

8) Explain the two types of segregation and give an example of each.
Page Ref: 113

9) Explain Edna Bonacich's split-labor-market theory.
Page Ref: 120-121

10) Discuss the motivation behind hate crimes.
Page Ref: 117-118

Chapter 5   Northern and Western Europeans

Multiple Choice Questions

1) During the colonial period, one of the most frequent causes of social problems was

   A) nationality.   B) religion.   C) race.   D) social class.

   Answer: B
   Page Ref: 129

2) The first European colonists had the which of the following in common?

   A) the necessity to survive   B) religious preference

   C) pro- or anti-British sentiments   D) all of the above

   Answer: D
   Page Ref: 130

3) Which of the following push factors motivated people to immigrate from their homeland?

   A) economic

   B) political

   C) religion

   D) adventure

   E) all of the above

   Answer: E
   Page Ref: 127

4) The civic culture included strong beliefs in

   A) Protestantism.

   B) Socialism.

   C) language bias.

   D) minority dominance.

   E) all of the above.

   Answer: A
   Page Ref: 130

5) Federalist action toward the increasing foreign-born population took the form of

   A) expulsion.   B) job discrimination.

   C) legislative controls.   D) spatial segregation.

   Answer: C
   Page Ref: 132

6) Between 1800 and 1850, which was <u>not</u> a characteristic of U.S. structural conditions in the settled regions?

   A) strong belief in Protestantism

   B) common culture based on the Anglo-Saxon model

   C) rapid growth of factories due to the Industrial Revolution

   D) way of life more stable and established

   Answer: C
   Page Ref: 133

7) The Know–Nothing movement of the 1850s illustrates

   A) acceptance.   B) avoidance.

   C) political apathy.   D) xenophobia.

   Answer: D
   Page Ref: 133–134

8) Many Federalists believed that the large foreign-born population was the root of all evil in the United States. This is an example of

   A) religious persecution.   B) economic opportunity.

   C) scapegoating.   D) their resistance to assimilation.

   Answer: C
   Page Ref: 132

9) Nineteenth–century British immigrants

   A) experienced widespread anti-British hostility.

   B) were the object of much ridicule on the vaudeville stage.

   C) clustered together in ethnic subcommunities.

   D) did not always like it here, and many returned home.

   Answer: D
   Page Ref: 138

10) New Amsterdam offers an early example of

   A) a pluralistic society.

   B) anti-Semitism.

   C) rigid social control.

   D) ethnocentrism.

   E) all of the above.

   Answer: A
   Page Ref: 140

11) Following 1820, shipmasters were required to

    A) file a directional plan.

    B) announce their ship's arrival.

    C) submit a passenger list to custom officials.

    D) expose passengers to the English language.

    E) none of the above

Answer: B
Page Ref: 133

12) Most immigrant groups were forced to live in substandard housing? The dominant group then argued that the new immigrants were dirty. This is an example of

    A) self-justification.   B) negative self-image.

    C) resistance to assimilation.   D) acculturation.

Answer: A
Page Ref: 133

13) New England French Canadians and Louisiana French illustrate

    A) amalgamation.   B) assimilation.

    C) convergent subcultures.   D) persistent subcultures.

Answer: D
Page Ref: 143

14) Franklin was opposed to the large German population in Pennsylvania because

    A) many were Mennonites and pacifists.   B) they were clannish.

    C) they had little knowledge of English.   D) all of the above

Answer: D
Page Ref: 146

15) The nineteenth-century German immigrants were

    A) diverse in religion, occupation, and area of residence.

    B) mostly lumberjacks living in the Midwest.

    C) mostly political refugees living in the eastern cities.

    D) mostly Sephardic Jews.

Answer: A
Page Ref: 146

16) Anxiety mounted between 1820 and 1860 because new German and Irish immigrants were

    A) Catholic.   B) Americanized.   C) illegal aliens.   D) violent..

Answer: A
Page Ref: 1133

17) Which Irish characteristic made them so unwelcome to many Americans?

    A) religion   B) peasant culture

    C) their strong anti-British feelings   D) all of the above

Answer: D
Page Ref: 149

18) Which societal reaction to their presence did the nineteenth-century Irish <u>not</u> experience?

    A) mob violence   B) job discrimination

    C) expulsion from certain cities   D) burning of churches and convents

Answer: C
Page Ref: 151

19) The Irish responded to their situation through

    A) avoidance.   B) deviance.

    C) defiance.   D) all of the above

Answer: D
Page Ref: 153

20) Which push factor was responsible for the majority of German immigrants?

    A) religion   B) economic

    C) political   D) none of the above

Answer: C
Page Ref: 147

21) Irish conflicts with Blacks, Chinese, and Germans all illustrate which theory?

    A) functionalism   B) internal colonialism

    C) marginality   D) split labor market

Answer: D
Page Ref: 162

22) Each of the immigrant groups brought food, music, traditions, etc. that are now part of the American culture. This is an example of

A) cultural diffusion.

B) assimilation.

C) cultural contagion.

D) amalgamation.

Answer: A
Page Ref: 148

23) The Scots offer a good example of

A) rapid assimilation.

B) persistent subculture.

C) social segregation.

D) negative self–image.

Answer: A
Page Ref: 159

24) The Welsh were primarily

A) factory workers.

B) farmers.

C) miners.

D) both B and C.

Answer: D
Page Ref: 159

25) Large groups of people arriving to forge a civilization on undeveloped land exemplifies the _____ perspective.

A) conflict

B) functionalist

C) interactionist

D) internal colonialism

Answer: B
Page Ref: 161

26) The nation's inability to absorb quickly the large numbers of Germans and Irish, resulting in a temporary societal disruption, illustrates which theory?

A) conflict

B) functionalist

C) interactionist

D) split labor market

Answer: B
Page Ref: 161

27) Federalist reaction to French and Irish immigrants illustrates which theory?

A) conflict

B) functionalist

C) interactionist

D) internal colonialism

Answer: A
Page Ref: 162

28) The brutal working conditions of the Irish for low wages illustrates which theory?

   A) conflict   B) functionalist

   C) interactionist   D) internal colonialism

   Answer: A
   Page Ref: 162

29) Contrasts among Dutch, Quaker, and Puritan responses to cultural pluralism illustrate

   A) conflict.

   B) functionalist.

   C) interactionist.

   D) split labor market.

   E) all of the above

   Answer: C
   Page Ref: 162

30) Protestant reaction to the large numbers of German Jews and Irish Catholics illustrates
   _____ theory.

   A) conflict   B) functionalist

   C) interactionist   D) internal colonialism

   Answer: C
   Page Ref: 163

True/False Questions

1) During the Colonial Period religious differences caused social problems more frequently than
   did nationality differences.

   Answer: TRUE
   Page Ref: 129

2) According to the 1790 census, one in every 10 people was a member of a racial minority.

   Answer: TRUE
   Page Ref: 130

3) The Alien and Sedition Acts were designed to encourage political activity by pro-French
   immigrants.

   Answer: FALSE
   Page Ref: 132

4) Urban living conditions, particularly among the poor Irish immigrants, were substandard.

   Answer: TRUE
   Page Ref: 133

5) U.S. citizens perceived the large influx of immigrants between 1820 and 1860 as a valuable contribution to the New World.

Answer: FALSE
Page Ref: 133

6) Push factors are the motivation behind emigration to a new location.

Answer: TRUE
Page Ref: 139–140

7) The Huguenots resisted assimilation until the late 1950s.

Answer: FALSE
Page Ref: 142

8) The emergence of television in the 1950s accelerated the process of ethnogenesis.

Answer: TRUE
Page Ref: 143

9) The Industrial Revolution brought rapid expansion to the New England factories.

Answer: TRUE
Page Ref: 144

10) Many German immigrants came to America with a team of indentured servants.

Answer: FALSE
Page Ref: 146

Essay Questions

1) What dominant and minority response patterns occurred during the colonial period?
Page Ref: 127–160

2) How did the open hostility between the WASPs and the new Irish and German immigrants first develop?
Page Ref: 1127

3) Explain how immigrants who were seeking religious freedom actually came to the New World with their own stereotyped beliefs. How did this impact their relationship with other immigrant groups?
Page Ref: 129

4) Explain fully the irony of many British immigrants finding the U.S. an undesirable place to remain.
Page Ref: 137–138

5) What aspect of the Dutch experience can we apply to that of current immigrant groups?

Page Ref: 138–141

6) Explain the roots of separation of church and state.

Page Ref: 130

7) What did Harriet Martineau, the "mother of sociology," mean when she said that the arrival of new immigrants was "a pure benefit"?

Page Ref: 1134–135

8) Explain Ralph Waldo Emerson's emphasis on the importance of the "smelting-pot."

Page Ref: 135

9) Why don't all immigrants desire to become full, participating citizens in the country to which they move?

Page Ref: 136

10) Contrast the three major sociological perspectives on the experiences of Northern and Western European immigrants.

Page Ref: 161–163

Chapter 6 Southern, Central, and Eastern Europeans

Multiple Choice Questions

1) The turning point when the total of immigrants from northern and western Europe was surpassed by the total from the rest of Europe occurred in

    A) 1880.   B) 1896.   C) 1901.   D) 1908.

Answer: B
Page Ref: 167

2) Which of the following was <u>not</u> a migration "pull" factor?

    A) job opportunities in industrial America

    B) quicker, sturdier, and inexpensive steamship travel

    C) harsh peasant life in Europe

    D) letters from friends and relatives already in America

Answer: C
Page Ref: 168

3) In 1880–1920, migration "push" factors included

    A) exploitation of the common people.   B) famine and poverty.

    C) political unrest.   D) all of the above.

Answer: D
Page Ref: 168

4) Working conditions at that time included

    A) long hours and low wages.   B) poor heating, lighting, and ventilation.

    C) child labor and unsafe machinery.   D) all of the above.

Answer: D
Page Ref: 170

5) According to Madison Grant's 1916 book, The Passing of the Great Race, the new influx of immigrants were faced with

    A) marginality   B) Anglo–conformity

    C) racism   D) ethnic hegemony

Answer: C
Page Ref: 171

6) Many believed rapid Americanization of the newcomers could be best achieved through

    A) the schools.   B) the churches.

    C) the government.   D) employment.

Answer: A
Page Ref: 174

7) The Haymarket Affair in 1886 set in motion which dominant group response pattern?

    A) expulsion   B) defiance   C) segregation   D) xenophobia

Answer: D
Page Ref: 175

8) The Dillingham Commission recommended what dominant group response pattern?

    A) legislative controls   B) forced assimilation

    C) segregation   D) expulsion

Answer: A
Page Ref: 176

9) Use of an immigrant quota system did not end until a new immigration law passed in 1965 called

    A) The Immigration and Nationality Act.   B) The McCarran–Walter Act.

    C) The Johnson–Reed Act.   D) The National Origins Quota Act.

Answer: A
Page Ref: 178

10) Slavs practiced child labor because of

    A) a value orientation that children were miniature adults.

    B) a value orientation about early vocational training.

    C) economic necessity.

    D) the unavailability of schools for their children.

Answer: C
Page Ref: 179

11) The study of Polish Americans by Thomas and Znaniecki showed that delinquency, divorce, prostitution, and crime were the result of

    A) a vigorous ethnic community.   B) family disorganization.

    C) a strong desire to assimilate.   D) low rates of crime and delinquency.

Answer: B
Page Ref: 181

12) Polish peasants viewed education as a waste of time and as a result they

A) trailed behind other groups in terms of upward mobility.

B) had an increase in upward mobility.

C) experienced stability, pride, and status competition.

D) all of the above

Answer: A
Page Ref: 182

13) Immigrants following the Bolshevik Revolution were most likely to be

A) Czarist army officers.   B) landowners.

C) professional people.   D) all of the above.

Answer: D
Page Ref: 183

14) Which of the following is closely associated with the xenophobic reaction to Russian immigrants?

A) assassination of President McKinley   B) lynch mobs

C) Palmer raids   D) Teapot Dome scandal

Answer: C
Page Ref: 184

15) Hungarians became prominent through their

A) productivity in farming.   B) participation in labor unrest.

C) failure to settle in ethnic clusters.   D) antilabor activity.

Answer: B
Page Ref: 188

16) Gypsies in the U.S. today can be described best as

A) virtually nonexistent.   B) fully assimilated.

C) a persistent subculture.   D) a convergent subculture.

Answer: C
Page Ref: 189

17) Gypsies have kept their tribal codes and morals virtually unchanged in an urbanized and industrialized society by

    A) remaining outside educational institutions.

    B) refusing to interact with strangers.

    C) living only in rural areas.

    D) all of the above.

Answer: A
Page Ref: 191

18) Many Italians participated in _____ patterns.

    A) shuttle migration   B) push migration

    C) train migration   D) permanent migration

Answer: A
Page Ref: 192

19) Italian immigrants continued to stress the value of

    A) individual achievement.   B) educational achievement.

    C) family cohesion.   D) formal education.

Answer: C
Page Ref: 194–195

20) Which term best identifies the status of second-generation Italian-Americans prior to 1940?

    A) marginality   B) rapid upward mobility

    C) geographic dispersion   D) college-educated

Answer: A
Page Ref: 195

21) Today, third and fourth generation Italian Americans are

    A) represented in the professional fields.

    B) attending colleges and universities in large numbers.

    C) becoming upwardly mobile.

    D) all of the above.

Answer: D
Page Ref: 196

22) An important social center for the Greek community was the

    A) village.   B) marketplace.   C) saloon.   D) coffeehouse.

Answer: D
Page Ref: 197

23) The Greek–American community has long demonstrated

    A) a blend of pluralistic and assimilationist patterns.

    B) low socioeconomic status.

    C) tightly clustered residential patterns.

    D) low value orientations about education.

Answer: A
Page Ref: 197

24) The Portuguese became a sizable portion of the working force

    A) on California's railroads.

    B) on Hawaii's pineapple and sugar plantations.

    C) in New England's mines.

    D) none of the above.

Answer: B
Page Ref: 199

25) The primary "push" factor for Armenian immigration to America was

    A) the genocidal campaign against them.   B) poverty.

    C) desire to conquer new lands.   D) none of the above

Answer: A
Page Ref: 201

26) Present day Armenian cohesion is based on

    A) the Armenian Apostolic Church.   B) strong family ties.

    C) family owned businesses.   D) both A and B.

Answer: D
Page Ref: 202

27) Which is the most accurate statement about immigrant women and work around 1890?

    A) Cultural norms dictated that married women should not work outside the home.

    B) About one–tenth of employed women worked in factories or mills.

    C) Most immigrant women workers were maids and nannies.

    D) both B and C

Answer: A
Page Ref: 203

28) Functional analysis would <u>not</u> include which of the following?

    A) influx of an extensive, unskilled labor pool

    B) behavioral pathologies after an abrupt life change

    C) perceptions of the newcomers by the native-born population

    D) society's ability to absorb massive numbers of immigrants

Answer: C
Page Ref: 204

29) Which statement accurately gives the conflict perspective for immigrants working for low wages under harsh conditions?

    A) They did not understand the language and customs.

    B) They were unaccustomed to an industrialized society.

    C) They fared better than living amidst European conflicts.

    D) Industrialists took advantage of them.

Answer: D
Page Ref: 205

30) Interactionist suggest a main reason for calls for immigration restrictions was the

    A) exploitation of the immigrants.

    B) association of the social problems with the new arrivals.

    C) rapid urban and industrial growth.

    D) overcrowding in schools.

Answer: B
Page Ref: 205

True/False Questions

1) The immigrants from southern, central and eastern Europe arrived in large enough numbers to be able to preserve some of their old-country culture.

Answer: TRUE
Page Ref: 167

2) Settling in the oldest city sections, immigrants quickly conformed to the dominant culture

Answer: FALSE
Page Ref: 169

3) According to Isaac A. Hourwich, World War I contributed to a redefinition of immigrant groups in nonracial terms.

Answer: TRUE
Page Ref: 173

4) The Johnson–Reed Act of 1924 was much less restrictive than The National Origins Quota Act of 1921.

Answer: FALSE
Page Ref: 177

5) Sojourners immigrated to America to earn money and then returned to their native land after a year or two.

Answer: TRUE
Page Ref: 179

6) Social segregation is normally a voluntary process.

Answer: FALSE
Page Ref: 179

7) A gemeinschaft society is regulated by custom and habit.

Answer: TRUE
Page Ref: 181

8) Greater individualism and less group cohesiveness often accompanied a climb up the socioeconomic ladder.

Answer: TRUE
Page Ref: 182

9) Many Russian Americans who had worked hard to achieve some economic security in the United States found themselves jobless and unable to find work after the Bolshevik Revolution in 1917.

Answer: TRUE
Page Ref: 184

10) The Displaced Persons Act called for the expulsion of any immigrant without familial ties in America.

Answer: FALSE
Page Ref: 186

Essay Questions

1) Describe the push–pull factors contributing to the increased immigration in 1880–1902.
Page Ref: 167–168

2) Discuss American's xenophobic reactions to the newcomers.
Page Ref: 171–178

3) Describe the structural conditions in which the new immigrants found themselves.
   Page Ref: 170

4) What were the findings and recommendations of the Dillingham Commission? What legislative action occurred?
   Page Ref: 176

5) Explain what Madison Grant meant when he said that "the vastly superior native U.S. stock was disappearing through 'racial suicide.'"
   Page Ref: 171

6) Discuss various aspects of Gypsy culture and why they continue to remain a persistent subculture.
   Page Ref: 189

7) In what ways do the Russians typify the experiences of other immigrant groups?
   Page Ref: 183–184

8) What similarities and dissimilarities can be found in the experiences of Italian and Greek immigrants?
   Page Ref: 191–198

9) Discuss the retention of cultural identity among many Portuguese and Armenians in the U.S.
   Page Ref: 198–199

10) Compare and contrast the three major sociological perspectives as they apply to the experiences of the groups discussed in this chapter.
   Page Ref: 204–206

Chapter 7 The Native Americans

Multiple Choice Questions

1) Native Americans experienced which of the following dominant group response patterns?

    A) legislative action

    B) segregation

    C) expulsion

    D) xenophobia

    E) all of the above

Answer: E
Page Ref: 211

2) Whites viewing Native Americans as cruel, treacherous, lying, dirty heathens is an example of

    A) self–justification.   B) discrimination.

    C) cruelty.   D) none of the above.

Answer: A
Page Ref: 212

3) Which is <u>not</u> a shared physical characteristic among most Native Americans?

    A) blue eyes   B) little facial or body hair

    C) prominent cheekbones   D) thick, straight, black hair

Answer: A
Page Ref: 212

4) In the mid–19th century, the U.S. government adopted a policy of _____ as a means to deal with Native Americans.

    A) xenophobia   B) ethnocentrism

    C) outgroup hostility   D) forced relocation

Answer: D
Page Ref: 212

5) Columbus's first impressions of the Arawak tribe in the Caribbean reflected

    A) xenophobia.   B) stereotyping.

    C) ethnocentrism.   D) self-justification.

Answer: C
Page Ref: 214

6) _____ viewed Native Americans as Noble Savages, while _____ viewed them as bloodthirsty barbarians.

    A) Bartolome de las Casas; Columbus

    B) Juan Gines de Sepulveda; Bartolome de las Casas

    C) Bartolome de las Casas; Juan Gines de Sepulveda

    D) Columbus; Juan Gines de Sepulveda

Answer: C
Page Ref: 217

7) For the Indian, cultural diffusion usually meant

    A) less self-sufficiency.   B) greater self-sufficiency.

    C) assimilation.   D) annihilation.

Answer: A
Page Ref: 219

8) Franklin's account of the Indian response to the offer of scholarships for educating Indian youth at Williamsburg illustrates

    A) assimilation.   B) different value orientations.

    C) integration.   D) upward mobility.

Answer: B
Page Ref: 219

9) An example of cultural diffusion from the Iroquois to the whites was their

    A) concept of land ownership.

    B) democratic resolution of differences in decision making.

    C) fondness for scalping.

    D) creating of a slave confederacy.

Answer: B
Page Ref: 220

10) Unrestrained displays of affection or temper and the use of corporal punishment have rarely been part of _____ child-care practices.

    A) the Europeans'   B) the Native Americans'

    C) the Greeks'   D) the Christians'

Answer: B
Page Ref: 221

11) The basic building blocks of Indian tribal society were

    A) intertribal alliances.   B) kin relationships.

    C) the buffalo.   D) ancestor worship.

Answer: B
Page Ref: 221

12) Belief that a wrong had to be repaid, even if it took years, but not to a greater degree is called

    A) self–justification.   B) ethnocentrism.

    C) retributive justice.   D) noncompetitive revenge.

Answer: C
Page Ref: 222

13) Native–American silence with strangers indicated

    A) caution.   B) aloofness.

    C) distrust of whites.   D) nonsociability.

Answer: A
Page Ref: 222

14) The expulsion of the Cherokee was primarily motivated by

    A) their inability to fit in with white society.

    B) their fertile land that was coveted by whites.

    C) the fact that they were a menace to the white settlements.

    D) all of the above

Answer: B
Page Ref: 227

15) The Trail of Tears refers to the deadly expulsion of the

    A) Cherokee.   B) Apache.   C) Iroquois.   D) Seminoles.

Answer: A
Page Ref: 228

16) The General Allotment Act of 1887 attempted to

    A) establish permanent Indian reservations.

    B) give individual allocations of food and clothing.

    C) offer employment assistance in urban centers.

    D) end communal ownership of Indian lands and encourage private ownership.

Answer: D
Page Ref: 229

17) One tribe brought to economic disaster by the termination program was the

   A) Cherokee.   B) Iroquois.   C) Menominee.   D) Taos Pueblo.

   Answer: C
   Page Ref: 231

18) The Native-American birthrate is

   A) almost twice the national average.

   B) slightly below the national average.

   C) below that of all other ethnic minorities.

   D) slowly decreasing.

   Answer: A
   Page Ref: 232

19) Efforts to overcome chronic unemployment among Native Americans now emphasize

   A) attracting light industry and business to reservations.

   B) increasing tourism to reservations.

   C) relocating Indians near industrial parks.

   D) creating a federal job corps.

   Answer: A
   Page Ref: 233

20) Suicide deaths among Native American youth are _____ the national average.

   A) more than twice   B) far below

   C) 50 percent greater than   D) 50 percent less than

   Answer: C
   Page Ref: 234

21) Investigating groups report education of Native-Americans

   A) will enable the next generation to enter the mainstream.

   B) is more effective at the boarding schools than elsewhere.

   C) has made great strides in reducing the drop-out rate.

   D) results in fewer high school graduates than for other U.S. minority groups.

   Answer: D
   Page Ref: 237

22) A recent proposed use for many reservations is as

  A) national parks.   B) tourist camping grounds.

  C) toxic dumping grounds.   D) independent municipalities.

Answer: C
Page Ref: 240

23) The nation's largest Indian reservation is that of the

  A) Arapahoe.   B) Navajo.   C) Osage.   D) Pueblo.

Answer: B
Page Ref: 241

24) The most serious resource shortage for many Western tribes is

  A) electricity.   B) fertilizer.   C) natural gas.   D) water.

Answer: D
Page Ref: 245

25) The Pan-Indian movement has been of limited success primarily because of

  A) emphasis on tribal identities.

  B) government resistance.

  C) reservations scattered among many states.

  D) weak leadership.

Answer: A
Page Ref: 246

26) The Alcatraz Proclamation was a

  A) government edict declaring the site to be Native-American land.

  B) sarcastic commentary on forced assimilation and reservation life.

  C) statement protesting violation of Native-American land rights.

  D) declaration of the establishment of Pan-Indianism.

Answer: B
Page Ref: 246

27) The 1973 Wounded Knee incident illustrates which minority-response pattern?

  A) annihilation   B) defiance   C) deviance   D) avoidance

Answer: B
Page Ref: 247

28) The major problem with the Bureau of Indian Affairs dealing with Native Americans is that

    A) no Native Americans are in leadership positions within the organization.

    B) the organization is not large enough to handle the many different tribes.

    C) it is a bureaucracy attempting to run people's lives.

    D) all of the above

Answer: C
Page Ref: 249

29) Urban Native Americans

    A) tend to settle in ethnic enclaves as have most immigrant groups.

    B) assimilate rather quickly and so are not a visible minority.

    C) may become acculturated but usually not assimilated.

    D) are extremely small in numbers.

Answer: C
Page Ref: 252

30) Which of the following words does NOT have its root in Native American language?

    A) tobacco   B) chipmunk   C) skunk   D) monkey

Answer: D
Page Ref: 252

True/False Questions

1) The ethnophaulism "redskins" is not at all accurate because Native Americans' skin coloring ranges from yellowish to coppery brown.

Answer: TRUE
Page Ref: 212

2) The least significant factor in the Native American's success was the civil rights movement.

Answer: FALSE
Page Ref: 214

3) Although he admired the Native Americans, Columbus essentially saw them as potential servants.

Answer: TRUE
Page Ref: 216

4) Juan Gines de Sepulveda convinced Spanish authorities that Africans were sturdier and better adapted to be agricultural workers than Native Americans.

Answer: FALSE
Page Ref: 217

5) Native American children grow up under the encouragement and discipline of the extended family, not just the nuclear family.

Answer: TRUE
Page Ref: 221

6) Native Americans first learned about scalping from the white settlers.

Answer: TRUE
Page Ref: 222

7) The Indian Removal Act recommended that all Native Americans in the northwestern states be relocated to the southeastern states.

Answer: FALSE
Page Ref: 224–225

8) After 1933, Franklin Roosevelt's administration shifted from a policy of forced assimilation to one of pluralism.

Answer: TRUE
Page Ref: 229

9) No research to date has found Native Americans to be different from other people regarding the physiology of alcohol metabolism.

Answer: TRUE
Page Ref: 235

10) Native Americans who leave their reservations and move to urban areas tend to be more successful than their peers who remain on the reservations.

Answer: FALSE
Page Ref: 251

Essay Questions

1) Discuss why Indian–white relations deteriorated from the peaceful early encounters.
Page Ref: 219

2) Explain how the Native Americans' view of nature differed from that of the white settlers.
Page Ref: 220–221

3) Discuss the social structure and child–rearing practices among many Indian tribes.
Page Ref: 221

4) Discuss fully the brutal treatment of the Cherokee in what was later called the Trail of Tears.
Page Ref: 228

5) Discuss three past federal programs, intended to promote assimilation, which further devastated the Indians.
Page Ref: 229–230

6) Describe the present living conditions on most reservations.
Page Ref: 232–240

7) Explain the current state of the reservations' natural resources?
Page Ref: 240–242

8) Explain some of the Red Power social movement efforts.
Page Ref: 245–247

9) Discuss some of the circumstances affecting the lives of urban Native Americans.
Page Ref: 249+251

10) Apply the three major sociological perspectives to the experiences of Native Americans.
Page Ref: 254–256

Chapter 8 East and Southeast Asian Americans

Multiple Choice Questions

1) Which of the following was a major social problem affecting most Asian immigrants up through the 1940s?

    A) alcoholism   B) suicide

    C) shortage of women   D) all of the above

Answer: C
Page Ref: 262

2) Generally, traditional Asian values emphasized which of the following

    A) appropriate behavior.

    B) strict control of aggressive or assertive impulses.

    C) self-conscious concern for conduct in the presence of others.

    D) all of the above

Answer: D
Page Ref: 263

3) Some ethnophaulisms about the Chinese dealt with their being

    A) industrious.   B) dirty.   C) quiet.   D) violent.

Answer: B
Page Ref: 265

4) The Chinese Exclusion Act of 1882 is significant because

    A) it was the first federal legislation against a particular race of immigrants.

    B) it was the first restrictive bill passed over a presidential veto.

    C) it was the first act to stop completely immigration from any one country.

    D) its passage brought organized labor into opposition with the government.

Answer: A
Page Ref: 267

5) Chinese immigrants utilized the minority group response of _____ when they formed Chinatowns.

    A) segregation   B) expulsion   C) xenophobia   D) rebellion

Answer: A
Page Ref: 268

6) In earlier years, the overabundance of chinese males and the scarcity of Chinese females let to

    A) organized prostitution.   B) deportation of males.

    C) return migration.   D) none of the above.

Answer: A
Page Ref: 272

7) It wasn't until the passage of the _____ that the Chinese were able to enter the U.S. under regular immigration regulations.

    A) Immigration Act of 1965   B) Burlingame Treaty of 1868

    C) Chinese Exclusion Act of 1882   D) all of the above

Answer: A
Page Ref: 272-273

8) Chinatowns today are

    A) declining in size, like many European ethnic communities.

    B) growing larger than in earlier years.

    C) primarily tourist attractions, not residential clusters.

    D) being replaced by Hispanic communities.

Answer: B
Page Ref: 273

9) A very recent example of deviance in the Chinese community is

    A) gambling.   B) tongs.

    C) brothels.   D) juvenile delinquency.

Answer: D
Page Ref: 274

10) Chinese Americans today are in which occupational fields?

    A) low-skill service workers   B) professional workers

    C) technical workers   D) all of the above

Answer: D
Page Ref: 274

11) A "push" factor spurring early Japanese migration was

    A) religious persecution.   B) political unrest.

    C) primogeniture.   D) famine.

Answer: C
Page Ref: 276

12) Many Japanese settled in rural areas instead of urban regions because

    A) labor union hostility prevented their finding much work in the cities.

    B) they came from an agrarian country and preferred farming.

    C) they did not get along with the Chinese who lived in the cities.

    D) they did not think cities were a good place to raise children.

    Answer: A
    Page Ref: 276

13) Which legislative effort prohibited any person who was ineligible for citizenship from owning land in California?

    A) Alien Landholding Law of 1913   B) Gentlemen's Agreement of 1908

    C) Immigration Act of 1965   D) all of the above

    Answer: A
    Page Ref: 276

14) One way the Gentlemen's Agreement improved the personal lives of U.S. Japanese was

    A) authorization of small business loans.

    B) permission for wives to enter the U.S.

    C) the right to own land.

    D) the liberalization of immigration regulations.

    Answer: B
    Page Ref: 277

15) Social scientists agree that the wartime incarceration of 110,000 Japanese–Americans was

    A) regrettable, but necessary for national security.

    B) a necessary form of protective custody against angry mobs.

    C) not racist–motivated.

    D) our worst wartime mistake.

    Answer: D
    Page Ref: 278

16) Japanese–Americans' emphasis on conformity, aspiration, competitiveness discipline, and self–control has resulted in

    A) changes in Japanese family structure and husband–wife roles.

    B) more rapid assimilation.

    C) increased opportunities due to resettlement.

    D) better school performance than other American students.

    Answer: D
    Page Ref: 281

17) About half of all new Japanese arrivals are

    A) skilled and professional workers.   B) blue collar workers.

    C) service industry workers.   D) blue collar and skilled workers.

Answer: A
Page Ref: 282

18) Japanese business people who come to the U.S. on two- or three-year assignments with their companies' U.S. branch offices are called

    A) sojourners.   B) return migrants.

    C) Kai-sha.   D) worker migrants.

Answer: C
Page Ref: 282

19) After the Gentlemen's Agreement Act of 1908 curtailed Japanese emigration, the Hawaiian Sugar Planters' Association recruited laborers from

    A) China.   B) the Philippines.

    C) Vietnam.   D) all of the above

Answer: B
Page Ref: 283

20) A major social problem for earlier Filipinos and a basis for societal hostility was

    A) widespread unemployment.   B) high alcoholism and suicide rates.

    C) the scarcity of Filipino women.   D) all of the above

Answer: C
Page Ref: 284

21) Since the Immigration Act of 1965, Filipino immigration has

    A) been quite high.   B) been severely restricted.

    C) stayed the same.   D) resulted in strict segregation.

Answer: A
Page Ref: 285

22) Early Korean immigrants were recruited by the

    A) railroad companies.   B) U.S. school system.

    C) petroleum industry leaders.   D) Hawaii Sugar Planters' Association.

Answer: D
Page Ref: 287

23) Koreans have utilized _____ to successfully immigrate to the U.S.

    A) sojourning   B) return migration

    C) chain–migration   D) segregation

Answer: A
Page Ref: 287

24) The greatest number of Korean immigrants came

    A) between 1903 and 1920.   B) between 1921 and 1949.

    C) between 1950 and 1969.   D) since 1970.

Answer: D
Page Ref: 287

25) High levels of church involvement among Korean immigrants was the result of

    A) marginalization.   B) religious beliefs.

    C) middle class status.   D) none of the above.

Answer: A
Page Ref: 288

26) *Phuc duc* is

    A) the belief in astrology as important in child–rearing practices.

    B) the amount of good fortune accumulated over generations of conduct.

    C) the belief in the ability to determine one's own fate.

    D) another term for reincarnation.

Answer: B
Page Ref: 290

27) Vietnamese refugees who possessed relatively traditional views faced the greatest culture shock and difficulty in adapting. This difficulty often resulted in

    A) depression.   B) anxiety.

    C) anger.   D) all of the above.

Answer: D
Page Ref: 292

28) During the secret war in Laos in the early 1970s, thousands of Hmong men and boys were recruited to

A) work for th e CIA.

B) fight in the military.

C) act as ambassadors for the U.S.

D) produce cameras and other types of monitoring equipment.

Answer: A
Page Ref: 296

29) In the late 1990s, anti-Asian violence

A) dropped significantly.

B) increased significantly.

C) remained virtually non-existent.

D) remained at about the same moderate level.

Answer: B
Page Ref: 297-298

30) Which is not a current pattern in Asian-American assimilation?

A) high family median income   B) low poverty rate

C) high racial intermarriage rate   D) high residential segregation

Answer: D
Page Ref: 299

True/False Questions

1) The Chinese first came to the United States during the California gold rush in the 1850s.

Answer: TRUE
Page Ref: 261

2) Legislators in all 50 states passed laws against miscegenation to prevent Asians from marrying whites.

Answer: FALSE
Page Ref: 262

3) Chinese laborers cost three times as much as whites for the railroad companies to maintain.

Answer: FALSE
Page Ref: 264-265

4) For more than 200 years, the Japanese had lived in government-enforced isolation.

Answer: TRUE
Page Ref: 275

5) In 1906, the San Francisco Board of Education created segregated "Oriental" schools.

Answer: TRUE
Page Ref: 277

6) Endo v. United States extended Japanese detention in relocation camps.

Answer: FALSE
Page Ref: 280-281

7) The Filipinos did not establish the support institutions usually found in immigrant communities.

Answer: TRUE
Page Ref: 285

8) New Filipino arrivals tend to have better educational and occupational skills than most of their ethnic cohorts born in the U.S.

Answer: TRUE
Page Ref: 285

9) Only 30 percent of the Korean American population identifies itself as Christian.

Answer: FALSE
Page Ref: 287

10) The self-employment rate of Korean Americans is the highest of all ethnic or racial groups.

Answer: TRUE
Page Ref: 289

Essay Questions

1) What West Coast conditions prompted racist attitudes and actions against Asian groups?
Page Ref: 265

2) Explain the concept of "yellow peril."
Page Ref: 266

3) Explain D. Y. Yuan's four-stage process of the development of Chinatowns.
Page Ref: 270

4) Explain the impact of the relocation centers on the Japanese American people.
Page Ref: 278-281

5) How did sex play a role in stirring racial hostility against the Chinese and Filipinos?
Page Ref: 283

6) Explain the "unique status" that Filipinos held in the U.S.
Page Ref: 283

7) Explain why Korean Americans have the highest self–employment rate of all ethnic and racial groups.
Page Ref: 289

8) Explain one of the main cultural differences between most people in the U.S. and the Vietnamese.
Page Ref: 290–291

9) Explain the "Model–Minority" stereotype that is associated with Asian Americans.
Page Ref: 298–299

10) Apply the three major sociological perspectives to the U.S. Asian experience.
Page Ref: 300–302

Chapter 9 Other Asian and Middle Eastern Americans

Multiple Choice Questions

1) Which is <u>not</u> often a push factor for nonwestern immigrants?

    A) overpopulation   B) poverty

    C) rapid air travel   D) government repression

Answer: C
Page Ref: 308

2) Today's non–Western immigrants usually differ from earlier ethnic groups in

    A) type of residential section.   B) job placement.

    C) acculturation patterns.   D) all of the above

Answer: D
Page Ref: 309

3) Many of today's professional Asian immigrants do not fit past acculturation patterns because they

    A) need not become Americanized to enjoy the lifestyle they want.

    B) have a religion different from the three major faiths.

    C) do not physically fit into the melting pot theory.

    D) do not fit into theories about behavior in the western world.

Answer: A
Page Ref: 309

4) Interaction surveys of Americans and nonwestern newcomers in professional, managerial, or technical fields show

    A) widespread social distance.

    B) much less social distance than in past years.

    C) extensive social distance for Africans but not Asians.

    D) extensive social distance for all but the Arabs.

Answer: A
Page Ref: 310

5) Most of the early Asian Indian immigrants were

    A) women and dependent children.

    B) male sojourners working as agricultural laborers.

    C) extended family groups.

    D) entire villages or communities.

Answer: B
Page Ref: 311

6) Which majority response was <u>not</u> experienced by Asian Indians in the early twentieth century?

    A) racial prejudice   B) housing discrimination

    C) forced assimilation   D) expulsion

Answer: C
Page Ref: 311–312

7) Asian Indians remaining in California through the 1950s, according to Hess, exemplified

    A) social stratification.   B) structural assimilation.

    C) a persistent subculture.   D) a convergent subculture.

Answer: C
Page Ref: 312–13

8) Which statement about Asian Indians is correct?

    A) Ease of population pressures has caused their emigration to decline.

    B) Exodus restrictions have caused their emigration to decline.

    C) Their immigration has been fairly constant since 1970.

    D) Asian-Indian population has increased dramatically in recent years.

Answer: D
Page Ref: 313

9) The push factors for Syrian immigrants included

    A) hunger and poverty.   B) disease.

    C) Turkish oppression.   D) all of the above.

Answer: D
Page Ref: 323

10) The occupation of _____ helped speed up Syrian acculturation.

    A) peddling   B) laborers   C) nursing   D) teaching

Answer: A
Page Ref: 325

11) Settlement patterning of recent Arab immigrants tends to be

    A) in tight clusters in the inner city.   B) widespread and in loose clusters.

    C) almost exclusively on the West Coast.   D) in rural and suburban areas.

Answer: B
Page Ref: 325

12) Most Palestinian Americans are

    A) Chritian.   B) Muslim.   C) Hindu.   D) Athiest.

Answer: B
Page Ref: 327

13) The local and regional association that assists Palestinian immigrants adjust to life in the U.S. is called

    A) chain migration.   B) Arab Nation.

    C) American Federation of Ramallah.   D) none of the above

Answer: C
Page Ref: 327

14) Most Iranians living in the U.S. in the late 1970s were

    A) political refugees.

    B) skilled professionals working as sojourners.

    C) religious refugees.

    D) none of the above.

Answer: B
Page Ref: 329

15) Settling in old city neighborhoods, the Syrians often replaced the

    A) Germans.   B) Irish.   C) Italians.   D) Jews.

Answer: B
Page Ref: 324

16) The term used for the gradual replacement in a neighborhood of one group by another is

    A) block-busting.   B) invasion-succession.

    C) migration.   D) gradated sequencing.

Answer: B
Page Ref: 324

17) Many Iranians kept to themselves for fear of

A) the SAVAK.

B) religious persecution.

C) violence.

D) none of the above.

Answer: A
Page Ref: 329

18) Syrian adjustment, acceptance, and upward mobility were fairly rapid because of their

A) wide dispersal which negated any significant opposition to their presence.

B) business expertise and self–employment.

C) middle–class values.

D) all of the above

Answer: D
Page Ref: 325

19) Syrian-Lebanese assimilation is nearly complete because they have entered what Milton Gordon calls the last stage, namely

A) financial security.

B) upward mobility.

C) large-scale intermarriage.

D) representation in all jobs and professions.

Answer: C
Page Ref: 326

20) Helping maintain the ethnic identity of the Palestinians living in the U.S. is their

A) language.

B) priests and churches.

C) political cause.

D) cultural institute program.

Answer: C
Page Ref: 327

21) The largest concentrations of Palestinian Americans is in

A) New York.

B) Maryland.

C) Michigan.

D) all of the above.

Answer: D
Page Ref: 327

22) A common social center for working-class Palestinian Americans is the

    A) neighborhood bar.   B) local coffeehouse.

    C) corner grocery store.   D) parish church.

Answer: B
Page Ref: 328

23) Iranian immigrants in the 1980s

    A) more than doubled the number from the 1970s.

    B) declined sharply because Iran refused to issue exit visas.

    C) declined sharply because of U.S.-Iran relations.

    D) continued the modest influx of the 1970s.

Answer: A
Page Ref: 330

24) Iranian Americans experiencing mixed feelings about no longer living in the homeland call themselves

    A) *mandegar.*   B) *belataklif.*   C) *slyasi.*   D) *Now-Ruz.*

Answer: B
Page Ref: 330

25) Today's second-generation Iranian Americans are mostly

    A) living in poverty.

    B) born to working-class parents.

    C) living in the southeastern U.S.

    D) born to middle-class professional parents.

Answer: D
Page Ref: 330

26) Sengstock found an Iraqi community in the Detroit area

    A) a persistent subculture despite changes in the homeland.

    B) changes in the homeland changing immigrant orientations.

    C) a village-oriented community nestled in an urban region.

    D) hostility against them because of the oil crisis.

Answer: B
Page Ref: 331

27) Turkish emigration to the U.S. was low because

   A) the U.S. was a Christian country.

   B) the traditional Turkish pattern of migration was of only large groups emigrating.

   C) Turkish law barred any emigrant from ever returning.

   D) all of the above

Answer: D
Page Ref: 332

28) Anti-Turkish sentiment in the U.S. prior to World War II was due primarily to

   A) the suppression and massacre of Armenians.

   B) the heroin traffic from Turkish poppy fields.

   C) anti-American actions in Turkey.

   D) Turkish support of the Russian pogroms.

Answer: A
Page Ref: 333

29) An important component of adjustment, acceptance, and assimilation is

   A) arranged marriages.   B) length of U.S. residence.

   C) older age at immigration.   D) recent visits to the country of origin.

Answer: B
Page Ref: 334

30) Someone stressing the undercurrents of resentment and tension against the visible presence of nonwestern minorities and their successes, probably reflects which perspective?

   A) conflict theory   B) functionalist theory

   C) interactionist theory   D) exchange theory

Answer: A
Page Ref: 336

True/False Questions

1) The third major wave of immigration occurred after 1965.

Answer: TRUE
Page Ref: 307–308

2) The early immigrants from the Middle East encountered much less discrimination than later immigrants.

Answer: FALSE
Page Ref: 310

3) Since the 1980s, less educated relatives of earlier immigrants have come to the U.S.

Answer: TRUE
Page Ref: 311

4) The San Francisco-based Asiatic Exclusion League quickly included Asian Indians among its targets.

Answer: TRUE
Page Ref: 311

5) In 1923 the U.S. Supreme Court ruled that Asian Indians were whites and thus eligible for citizenship.

Answer: FALSE
Page Ref: 312

6) "Little Arabia is located in Dearborn, Michigan.

Answer: TRUE
Page Ref: 317

7) Many of today's Arab Americans are less sophisticated than other middle-class U.S. citizens.

Answer: FALSE
Page Ref: 319

8) Syrian males usually came alone and then sent for their wives and children.

Answer: TRUE
Page Ref: 324

9) Most Palistinian Americans are Hindus.

Answer: FALSE
Page Ref: 327

10) Although immigration officials identified them as Turkish by their passports, they really were Armenians, Syrians, Lebanese, or other nationalities.

Answer: TRUE
Page Ref: 332

Essay Questions

1) Who is involved in the third major wave of immigration?
Page Ref: 307-308

2) Discuss some of the push-pull factors and acculturation problems affecting Asian-Indian immigrants.
Page Ref: 3308

3) Describe some differences between early and recent Asian Indian and Middle Eastern immigrants.

Page Ref: 309

4) How does the residential patterning and community life of today's Arab Americans differ from that of past European immigrants?

Page Ref: 320

5) How did September 11, 2001 impact the acceptance of Arab Muslims?

Page Ref: 310

6) Explain the impact of miscegenation laws on Asian Indians.

Page Ref: 319

7) Explain the role of the National Association of Arab Americans and the Association of Arab American University Graduates in adjustment of Arab immigrants.

Page Ref: 373

8) What types of Arab stereotypes existed before and after September 11, 2001?

Page Ref: 321

9) Discuss Ansari's four self-designated categories of Iranians.

Page Ref: 330

10) Apply the three major sociological perspectives to the experiences of the groups discussed in this chapter.

Page Ref: 335-336

Chapter 10 Black Americans

Multiple Choice Questions

1) Racism emerged as an ideology

    A) after slavery began in the U.S.

    B) sometime in the sixteenth and seventeenth centuries.

    C) during the sectional rivalry in the early nineteenth century.

    D) only in the twentieth century.

Answer: B
Page Ref: 343

2) Myths about Black racial inferiority

    A) began with the ancient Egyptians.

    B) originated in Africa to discourage the slave trade.

    C) emerged as a rationalization for U.S. slavery.

    D) were rejected by slave owners who knew Blacks worked hard.

Answer: C
Page Ref: 343

3) The gradual and pervasive change in the values of a people is known as

    A) value shift.   B) cultural drift.

    C) cultural differentiation.   D) value evolution.

Answer: B
Page Ref: 345

4) The principle of "separate but equal" was

    A) upheld by the Supreme Court in the 1896 Plessy v. Ferguson ruling.

    B) struck down by the Supreme Court in 1896.

    C) recommended by President Lincoln.

    D) created by Congress in 1896 with passage of the Plessy–Ferguson Act.

Answer: A
Page Ref: 346

5) Myrdal called the intensification of discrimination resulting from Jim Crow laws

    A) exponential pathology.   B) cumulative causation.

    C) behavioral rigidity.   D) societal racism.

Answer: B
Page Ref: 348

6) In the early twentieth century, the migration of southern blacks to the North was due mostly to

    A) the existence of Jim Crow laws and poor economic conditions in the South.

    B) better educational opportunities in the North.

    C) more political freedom in the North.

    D) all of the above.

Answer: D
Page Ref: 348

7) In the 1920s, the Ku Klux Klan spread northward and

    A) added Jews, Catholics, and foreigners to its list of targets.

    B) focused on the urban blacks who had migrated from the South.

    C) were ignored by almost everyone.

    D) seized control of several state legislatures.

Answer: A
Page Ref: 350

8) In 1954, the landmark desegregation order covered

    A) schools only.

    B) transportation only.

    C) any public establishment.

    D) any form of segregation, including housing.

Answer: A
Page Ref: 351

9) The 1960s sit-ins and freedom rides are examples of which minority response pattern?

    A) avoidance   B) defiance

    C) deviance   D) self-justification

Answer: B
Page Ref: 353

10) The measurable impact of the massive civil rights legislation was its

    A) changing of people's attitudes.

    B) creation of the welfare system.

    C) provision of equal life opportunities for African Americans.

    D) exclusion of Native Americans.

Answer: C
Page Ref: 355

11) Since the mid–1960s, the number of elected black officials has

    A) increased slightly.

    B) increased dramatically.

    C) decreased slightly because of Hispanic immigration.

    D) decreased dramatically because of Asian immigration.

Answer: B
Page Ref: 356

12) The National Commission on Civil Disorders said a major cause of the 1960s riots was

    A) police practices.

    B) unemployment and underemployment.

    C) inadequate housing.

    D) all of the above

Answer: D
Page Ref: 357

13) The 1992 Los Angeles riot

    A) was a black versus white riot like the 1965 Watts riot.

    B) did not involve Latinos.

    C) was a black versus white and Korean riot.

    D) was a multiracial riot with various conflict combinations.

Answer: D
Page Ref: 358

14) *The Bell Curve* says the best explanation of wealth, status, poverty, and social pathologies is

    A) education.   B) intelligence.

    C) occupation.   D) the work ethic.

Answer: B
Page Ref: 359

15) Critics attack *The Bell Curve* for its

    A) selective use of data.   B) poor scholarship and methodology.

    C) questionable analytical techniques.   D) all of the above

Answer: D
Page Ref: 359

16) The major criticism against using intelligence testing to compare the capabilities of races is

    A) the presumption that genetic factors explain differences in scores.

    B) the presumption that cultural factors explain differences in scores.

    C) no significant or consistent differences in scores occur.

    D) whites outnumber blacks, giving them an unfair advantage.

Answer: A
Page Ref: 360–361

17) Words may subconsciously encourage racial prejudgment because

    A) they are nasty words.   B) if you hear them, you believe them.

    C) of their negative connotations.   D) of their frequent repetition.

Answer: C
Page Ref: 362

18) Population movement since 1960 from inside to outside central cities

    A) involved few African Americans.

    B) reduced the percentage of African Americans living outside central cities.

    C) kept the proportion of African Americans living outside central cities fairly constant.

    D) almost doubled the percentage of African Americans living outside central cities.

Answer: D
Page Ref: 367–368

19) Analysis of the age distribution of American blacks and whites shows

    A) blacks have a larger percentage of young people.

    B) whites have a larger percentage of young people.

    C) a fairly even age distribution between the two races.

    D) both blacks and whites are experiencing a new "baby boom."

Answer: A
Page Ref: 362

20) In level of educational achievement, blacks

    A) are further behind whites than before 1954.

    B) are no different now overall than before 1954.

    C) have narrowed the gap between the races completing four years of high school.

    D) are now equal to whites.

Answer: C
Page Ref: 363

21) In terms of income, which group has benefited most from all the civil rights actions?

    A) black poor

    B) black middle class

    C) both the black poor and the black middle class

    D) neither the black poor nor the black middle class

Answer: B
Page Ref: 366

22) Blauner's "internal-colonialism" refers to

    A) the rise in tenement housing.

    B) the large number of African Americans trapped in ghettos.

    C) racial pride.

    D) both B and C.

Answer: B
Page Ref: 366

23) The fastest growing segment of the population living in poverty is

    A) farm laborers.   B) laid-off city employees.

    C) female-headed families.   D) black social workers.

Answer: C
Page Ref: 366

24) Black men are more likely than white men to be employed as

    A) firefighters.   B) policemen.

    C) food-service workers.   D) all of the above.

Answer: D
Page Ref: 366

25) Wilson maintains that denial of upward mobility to the black poor results from

    A) social class barriers that limit life chances.

    B) racial discrimination.

    C) cutbacks in government support programs.

    D) job competition from Hispanic immigrants.

Answer: A
Page Ref: 370–371

26) Which statement is correct about the black middle class?

    A) Their earnings are comparable to the white middle class.

    B) Their businesses are less susceptible to failure because of government aid.

    C) They still endure various forms of racism.

    D) all of the above

Answer: C
Page Ref: 372

27) Which of the following statements regarding current black immigration is correct?

    A) African immigration is virtually nonexistent.

    B) A small trickle of African immigrants come each year.

    C) African immigration has been steadily declining since European colonial rule ended.

    D) African immigration has been significantly increasing in recent years.

Answer: D
Page Ref: 374

28) African immigrants and black Americans

    A) identify with each other because of the racial bond.

    B) seldom interact because of the cultural differences.

    C) are alike, since both are African Americans.

    D) come into frequent conflict with one another.

Answer: B
Page Ref: 373

29) Immigration from Haiti will likely

    A) continue for a long time.

    B) be limited in number and duration.

    C) surpass that from Mexico.

    D) eliminate all problems related to poverty.

Answer: A
Page Ref: 375

30) African-born Americans

    A) tend to be better educated than American-born African Americans.

    B) tend to have higher income levels than American-born African Americans

    C) tend to own their homes in greater numbers than American-born African Americans.

    D) all of the above

Answer: D
Page Ref: 377

True/False Questions

1) Most Africans who arrived in America from 1619 until the end of the slave trade, in 1808, immigrated unwillingly.

Answer: TRUE
Page Ref: 341

2) Similarity in culture have helped create a unifying racial bond between black immigrants and native-born blacks.

Answer: FALSE
Page Ref: 341

3) To ease their transition to a new land, other ethnic groups re-created in miniature the society they left behind; but the Africans who came to the Unites States were not allowed to do so.

Answer: TRUE
Page Ref: 342

4) "Black codes" were state laws designed to prevent blacks from being forced back into slavery.

Answer: FALSE
Page Ref: 345

5) Institutionalized racism occurs when laws attempt to legitimize differential racial treatments.

Answer: TRUE
Page Ref: 345

6) Although African Americans found greater freedom in the North, the dominant group's animosity toward them led to majority patterns of avoidance and discrimination.

Answer: TRUE
Page Ref: 349

7) Although popular in the 19th century, today the Ku Klux Klan is considered a relic from the past.

Answer: FALSE
Page Ref: 350–351

8) Rosa Parks' refusal to sit at the back of the bus eventually led the Federal District Court to rule against segregated seating.

Answer: TRUE
Page Ref: 351–352

9) The term "white flight" refers to the significant white lower–class migration from the suburbs to the inner cities.

Answer: FALSE
Page Ref: 358–359

10) Racial segregation remains stubbornly rooted in the nation's older cities, where blacks and whites have always lived apart.

Answer: TRUE
Page Ref: 370

Essay Questions

1) What is meant by the legacy of racism and slavery?
Page Ref: 343

2) Discuss and illustrate the concept of language as prejudice.
Page Ref: 362

3) Discuss the Jim Crow laws as examples of cultural drift.
Page Ref: 345–346

4) Discuss the legacy and subtlety of racism.
Page Ref: 345

5) Explain Gunnar Myrdal's conclusion that "discrimination breeds discrimination."
Page Ref: 348

6) Explain the two phases of desegregation.
Page Ref: 351–356

7) Discuss the current debate of race versus social class as a basis for understanding the current status of race relations.
Page Ref: 370–371

8) What factors contributed to the cooling of black urban violence?
Page Ref: 357

9) Discuss the various reasons for diversity in the black assimilation process.
Page Ref: 378–379

10) Apply the three major sociological perspectives to the black experience in the U.S.
Page Ref: 379–382

Chapter 11 Hispanic Americans

Multiple Choice Questions

1) Variances in the Hispanic experience in the U.S. are due to

    A) differences among the Hispanic peoples.

    B) time periods in which the immigrants arrived.

    C) regions in which they settled.

    D) all of the above

Answer: D
Page Ref: 387

2) The Treaty of Guadalupe Hidalgo ended the Mexican-American War in 1848 and brought _____ into the United States.

    A) Texas

    B) New Mexico

    C) Arizona

    D) California

    E) all of the above

Answer: E
Page Ref: 387-388

3) *La Raza Cosmica* refers to

    A) an annual competitive event among Hispanic peoples.

    B) a common bond and great destiny for the Hispanic peoples.

    C) a master-race concept asserting Hispanics are superior.

    D) the emphasis upon nuclear, not extended, families.

Answer: B
Page Ref: 390

4) In the U.S., the culture clash regarding machismo is

    A) the stereotype of a woman as a sex object.

    B) the belief in male dominance and female submissiveness.

    C) less opportunity for males to display physical prowess.

    D) the emphasis upon nuclear, not extended, families.

Answer: B
Page Ref: 390-391

5) *Dignidad* refers to

A) reciprocal respect in human interaction.

B) formal rules of etiquette.

C) deference to those of high status.

D) all of the above.

Answer: A
Page Ref: 391

6) Which of the following statements about Latin American countries is the most correct?

A) Racial prejudice is nonexistent.

B) Social class, not race, is the primary basis for differential treatment.

C) A sharp racial line determines social standing.

D) Racial prejudice is worse than in the U.S.

Answer: B
Page Ref: 391

7) Which term best describes most Hispanic Americans today?

A) cultural hegemony   B) Americanization

C) pluralism   D) structural assimilation

Answer: C
Page Ref: 394

8) Mexican Americans may be described as

A) nonassimilable because of their proximity to Mexico.

B) confined almost exclusively to the American Southwest.

C) a single group of mostly impoverished workers.

D) diverse in values, socioeconomic status, and assimilation.

Answer: D
Page Ref: 395

9) "Repatriation" and "Operation Wetback" are examples of

A) expulsion.   B) forced assimilation.

C) Americanization.   D) self-justification.

Answer: A
Page Ref: 400–401

10) The Zoot Suit Riots of 1943 illustrate

    A) dominant-group tolerance of violence against a minority.

    B) an extreme form of minority-group defiance.

    C) labor unrest in times of economic trouble.

    D) the failure of government-mandated hiring programs.

Answer: A
Page Ref: 402

11) Mexican Americans in Los Angeles and New Mexico, compared to those living elsewhere,

    A) are less likely to enter the mainstream of U.S. society.

    B) exhibit a greater retention of their culture.

    C) show a greater degree of assimilation.

    D) live mostly in the poorest sections of the cities.

Answer: C
Page Ref: 403

12) Current stereotypes regarding Mexican Americans include

    A) gang members.   B) lazy.

    C) illegal aliens.   D) all of the above.

Answer: D
Page Ref: 403

13) Chicano power was promoted by

    A) Cesar Chavez.   B) David Sanchez.

    C) Rodolfo Tijerina.   D) all of the above.

Answer: D
Page Ref: 404

14) In the early twentieth century, U.S. policy toward Puerto Rico was

    A) mostly to encourage economic investment.

    B) simply exploitation.

    C) an attempt at Americanization.

    D) introduction of pluralism.

Answer: C
Page Ref: 406

15) Changes in the U.S. economy affect Puerto Rico because

    A) most of its labor force works on the mainland.

    B) it is only a small island.

    C) of its economic dependency on the U.S.

    D) all of the above

Answer: C
Page Ref: 407

16) In Puerto Rico, as in all Latin American countries, an individual's identity, importance, and security depend on

    A) migration patterns.   B) family membership.

    C) religion.   D) occupation.

Answer: B
Page Ref: 408

17) Which does <u>not</u> reduce Puerto Rican involvement in the Catholic Church on the mainland?

    A) outgroup representation in the church hierarchy

    B) inability to internalize a Catholic identity

    C) the appeal of Pentecostal churches

    D) spiritualism and superstition

Answer: B
Page Ref: 409

18) In the Puerto Rican American communities, bodegas serve as

    A) religious temples.   B) hair salons.

    C) social gathering places.   D) a source of cultural pride.

Answer: C
Page Ref: 411

19) Puerto Ricans surpass Mexican Americans in all of the following categories except

    A) fluency in English.   B) educational level.

    C) proportion not living in poverty.   D) length of residence in mainland U.S.

Answer: C
Page Ref: 412

20) Through the _____ the United States reserved the right to intervene in Cuba if necessary to protect U.S. interests.

    A) Know–Nothing Party   B) Labor Unions

    C) Platt Amendment   D) Peace Act Agreement

Answer: C
Page Ref: 413

21) Cuban cultural values emphasize all but which of these?

    A) live in order to work and achieve physical comfort

    B) redirect hostility into humor and wit

    C) readily display kindness and generosity

    D) avoid being unwitty or disagreeable

Answer: A
Page Ref: 415–416

22) Compared to other Hispanic–American groups, Cubans have

    A) greater educational attainment.   B) a lower unemployment rate.

    C) a higher median family income.   D) all of the above.

Answer: D
Page Ref: 416–417

23) Dominicans commonly co–exist in neighborhoods alongside those of the

    A) Cubans.   B) Mexicans.   C) Nicaraguans.   D) Puerto Ricans.

Answer: D
Page Ref: 418

24) The sanctuary movement that hid Salvadoran refugees from immigration officials involved

    A) Catholic clergy and parishioners.

    B) Cubans serving as a middleman minority.

    C) Mexican smugglers.

    D) the Underground Railroad.

Answer: A
Page Ref: 420

25) The greatest number of South American immigrants come from

    A) Argentina.   B) Chile.   C) Colombia.   D) Ecuador.

Answer: C
Page Ref: 421

26) A significant variable in Hispanic immigrant youth remaining in school is their

    A) age at the time of entry into the U.S.   B) attendance.

    C) size of family.   D) living in a two–parent household.

Answer: A
Page Ref: 422

27) What groups have low intermarriage rates with non–Hispanics?

    A) Central and South Americans   B) Cubans and Mexicans

    C) Dominicans and Puerto Ricans   D) Colombians and Peruvians

Answer: C
Page Ref: 423–424

28) According to functional analysis,

    A) the Hispanic community is unimportant in adjustment to U.S. life.

    B) Cuban revitalization of neighborhoods has hurt other Hispanic groups.

    C) allowing an underclass undermines personal rights and equal opportunities.

    D) existence of a dual economy denies job opportunities to Hispanics.

Answer: C
Page Ref: 424–425

29) According to conflict analysis, improvement of Hispanic status depends upon their

    A) learning the English language.

    B) developing political power.

    C) benefiting from greater government jobs programs.

    D) reduced immigration to stabilize their ethnic communities.

Answer: B
Page Ref: 425

30) According to interactionist analysis, Anglos

    A) have good awareness of Hispanic diversity because of television.

    B) are highly receptive to Hispanic pluralism.

    C) apply understandings of European immigrant patterns to the Hispanics.

    D) often misinterpret Hispanic ethnicity and behavior.

Answer: D
Page Ref: 426

True/False Questions

1) Puerto Ricans became U.S. nationals when the Treaty of Paris in 1898 ended the Spanish–American War.

Answer: TRUE
Page Ref: 388

2) Undocumented aliens make substantial economic contributions as consumers and low–skilled worker.

Answer: TRUE
Page Ref: 390

3) Marianismo is an organization of women who have come together to protest male patterns of machismo.

Answer: FALSE
Page Ref: 391

4) Hispanics generally have a more casual attitude toward time than do others in the United States.

Answer: TRUE
Page Ref: 392

5) Hispanics are the largest ethnic group in the United States and are steadily increasing in number all the time.

Answer: TRUE
Page Ref: 392

6) Housing is the most important indicator of societal mainstreaming.

Answer: FALSE
Page Ref: 395

7) The median family income for Latino families has traditionally been higher than for black families.

Answer: TRUE
Page Ref: 398

8) In the second half of the 19th century, Mexicans from south of the border helped fill U.S. labor needs for the construction of railroad lines and the expansion of cotton, fruit, and vegetable farms.

Answer: TRUE
Page Ref: 400

9) The bracero program encouraged American-born Hispanics to sponsor recent immigrants to the U.S.

Answer: FALSE
Page Ref: 400

10) Puerto Ricans refer to their island as the "true melting pot."

Answer: TRUE
Page Ref: 405

Essay Questions

1) Explain the Hispanic concepts of *dignidad, machismo,* and *La Raza Cosmica.*
Page Ref: 390–391

2) Contrast prevailing racial attitudes in Latin America and in the U.S.
Page Ref: 391

3) Explain two negative dominant-response patterns against Mexicans in the twentieth century.
Page Ref: 400–401

4) What prevented the Catholic Church from being an effective social force for Puerto Ricans as it once was for other groups?
Page Ref: 408–409

5) Discuss the fallacy of Mexican stereotypes.
Page Ref: 403–404

6) Explain the cultural and historical factors that Fitzpatrick said led to more tolerant racial attitude in Puerto Rico.
Page Ref: 406

7) Explain why Puerto Ricans have the highest poverty rate of any major racial or ethnic group.
Page Ref: 411–412

8) Discuss the rise of Chicano Power since the 1960s.
Page Ref: 404–405

9) What assimilation patterns do we currently find among Hispanics in the social institutions of family and education?
Page Ref: 422–423

10) Apply the three major sociological perspectives to the Hispanic experience in the U.S.
Page Ref: 424–426

Chapter 12   Religious Minorities

Multiple Choice Questions

1) The number of religious groups in the U.S. today numbers

    A) under 500.   B) about 1,000.   C) over 1,500.   D) over 2,000.

Answer: C
Page Ref: 433

2) According to Miller, Americans are leaving mainstream churches in droves to join

    A) cults.   B) megachurches.

    C) nondenominational churches.   D) both B and C.

Answer: D
Page Ref: 433

3) Throughout much of the colonial period, U.S. Catholics

    A) encountered discriminatory laws in all thirteen colonies.

    B) faced no discriminatory laws since they were so few in number.

    C) settled mostly in New England where people were more hospitable.

    D) dominated Maryland which was their power base at the Constitutional Convention.

Answer: A
Page Ref: 435–436

4) A late nineteenth century anti-Catholic organization with over 500,000 members was the

    A) American Protective Association.   B) Anti-Catholic Citizens League.

    C) Catholic Exclusion Alliance.   D) Patriots Against Romanism.

Answer: A
Page Ref: 436

5) Which of the following did <u>not</u> generate Protestant hostility against American Catholics?

    A) building of convents and parochial schools

    B) church doctrine and hierarchy

    C) individual interpretation of the Bible

    D) celibacy of priests and nuns

Answer: C
Page Ref: 437

6) The greatest conflict between Catholics and Protestants was on the subject of

A) tax exemption status.
B) education.
C) zoning variances for convents.
D) Sunday blue laws.

Answer: B
Page Ref: 438

7) U.S. Catholics today are

A) less than ten percent of the total population.

B) declining in numbers, except for Hispanic immigrant additions.

C) more than 50 percent of the total population.

D) the largest single religious denomination in the U.S.

Answer: D
Page Ref: 438

8) Anti-Jewish stereotypes included

A) scoundrels.

B) comic characters.

C) clannish.

D) pushy.

E) all of the above.

Answer: E
Page Ref: 441

9) Achieving economic success but not public acceptance is known as

A) social ostracism.
B) clannishness.
C) parasitic deference.
D) consciousness of kind.

Answer: A
Page Ref: 443

10) Many Jewish immigrants were aided in achieving fairly rapid upward mobility by

A) their clannishness and conspiratorial help for one another.

B) their job skills and values.

C) their familiarity with the English language.

D) all of the above.

Answer: B
Page Ref: 442

11) What strained relations between the "old" Jewish population and the "new" Jewish arrivals?

    A) ethnic and nationalist prejudices   B) social class differences

    C) religious differences   D) all of the above

Answer: D
Page Ref: 440

12) Often accompanying Jewish economic success was

    A) social segregation.   B) structural assimilation.

    C) return to their native land.   D) social acceptance.

Answer: A
Page Ref: 443

13) The percentage of Jews marrying Christians

    A) remains low, less than ten percent.

    B) is decreasing rather steadily, about one percent each year.

    C) has been rather consistent over the years, about 20 percent annually.

    D) has been increasing rapidly, now exceeding 50 percent.

Answer: D
Page Ref: 444

14) What primary motivation prompted the Mormons to move westward from New York?

    A) economic opportunity   B) expulsion

    C) overpopulation   D) railroad work

Answer: B
Page Ref: 446–447

15) Migration in 1847 to the Great Salt Lake Valley resulted from

    A) the threat of extermination or forced assimilation.

    B) the lure of gold and silver discoveries.

    C) the desire to live in a less settled region.

    D) an avoidance response to the growing slavery issue.

Answer: A
Page Ref: 447

16) What federal government action against Mormons did <u>not</u> occur?

    A) military warfare   B) confiscation of church property

    C) imprisonment for lewd cohabitation   D) removal from political office

Answer: D
Page Ref: 447

17) Which of the following is <u>not</u> forbidden among Mormons?

    A) alcoholic beverages   B) coffee or tea

    C) smoking   D) women working

Answer: D
Page Ref: 447–448

18) Mormon values stress which of the following?

    A) educational achievement   B) family togetherness

    C) economic interdependence   D) all of the above

Answer: D
Page Ref: 448

19) Islam incorporates many beliefs and practices of

    A) Buddhism and Hinduism.   B) Buddhism and Christianity.

    C) Christianity and Judaism.   D) Christianity and Hinduism.

Answer: C
Page Ref: 451–452

20) Muslims are concerned about which of the following interfering with their ability to maintain the integrity of their way of life?

    A) pornography.

    B) divorce.

    C) alcohol and drug abuse.

    D) abortions.

    E) all of the above.

Answer: E
Page Ref: 452–453

21) A common aspect of all Amish communities is their

    A) beautiful country churches.

    B) adaptability to modern life.

    C) high degree of integration and harmony.

    D) dependence on tourism.

Answer: C
Page Ref: 454

22) Symbols of Amish group identity include all but which of the following?

A) clothing

B) language

C) specially styled jewelry

D) knowledge of High German

Answer: C
Page Ref: 454

23) Which sentence is most correct?

A) The Amish demand conservative behavior from their teenagers.

B) The Amish permit adolescent rebelliousness prior to adult church membership.

C) The Amish permit their teenagers to date outgroup members.

D) The Amish emphasize educational achievement through high school only.

Answer: B
Page Ref: 455

24) Rastafarians believe themselves to be

A) black Israelites.

B) black Muslims.

C) black Arabs.

D) black Indians.

Answer: A
Page Ref: 458

25) Which is part of the Rastafarian behavior code?

A) emphasis on frequent shampooing to maintain dreadlocks

B) using only natural foods without chemical processing

C) drinking only natural milk, not liquor or soda

D) using "you" and "me" only when speaking to outgroup members

Answer: B
Page Ref: 459

26) Santeria in the U.S. today is

A) exclusively followed by Hispanics.

B) a highly ethnocentric Cuban religion.

C) against any form of animal sacrifice.

D) a multi-ethnic, multi-racial, secret religion.

Answer: D
Page Ref: 461

27) Which statement is correct?

   A) Hindus are vegetarians.

   B) Hindus believe in three gods.

   C) Hindus can practice another religion simultaneously.

   D) all of the above

Answer: C
Page Ref: 463

28) Which of the following social castes is considered to be the elite?

   A) Brahmins

   B) Kshatriyas

   C) Vaishyas

   D) Sudras

   E) Harijan

Answer: A
Page Ref: 463

29) Controversies over abortion and school prayer

   A) once again pit Protestants against Catholics.

   B) are illustrations of civil religion.

   C) unite people of many different faiths in a common cause.

   D) threaten to create deep religious division in the country.

Answer: C
Page Ref: 466

30) Creationists' support for a literal interpretation of the Bible puts them in conflict with which of the following theories?

   A) Big Bang

   B) Red Shift

   C) Isotope decay and carbon dating

   D) Evolutionary

   E) all of the above

Answer: E
Page Ref: 467

True/False Questions

1) The U.S. is now probably the most religiously diverse country in the world.

Answer: TRUE
Page Ref: 433

2) Religious differences fan the flames of intense bigotry and acts of mob violence in the U.S.

Answer: FALSE
Page Ref: 433–434

3) The Guardians of Liberty were dedicated to keeping Catholics out of office because they would supposedly take their orders from Rome.

Answer: TRUE
Page Ref: 437

4) U.S. Protestants considered vows of celibacy among priests and nuns unnatural.

Answer: TRUE
Page Ref: 437–438

5) According to the Council of Jewish Federations, 75 percent of the children from mixed marriages are brought up as Jews.

Answer: FALSE
Page Ref: 444

6) Many Jewish Americans today see religion less as an inherited ethnic identity and more as a personal choice of belief and practice.

Answer: TRUE
Page Ref: 445

7) The discovery of silver in California ended Mormon isolation because their settlement was located along the best route to the California silver mines.

Answer: FALSE
Page Ref: 447

8) Mormons take care of their own poor, without public-welfare assistance.

Answer: TRUE
Page Ref: 449

9) Although Westerners may think of Islam as an Arab religion, most Muslims throughout the world are not Arabs.

Answer: TRUE
Page Ref: 451

10) The Amish support social security and all other forms of insurance, believing the country should be responsible for its people.

Answer: FALSE
Page Ref: 456

Essay Questions

1) Describe the role of the clergy in an immigrant group's adjustment to their new home in the U.S.
Page Ref: 435

2) Explain the impact of the ecumenical movement on the Catholic religion.
Page Ref: 438

3) Compare and contrast the first three waves of Jewish immigrants to the U.S.
Page Ref: 439

4) Discuss some of the cultural factors that contributed to the success of some first- and many second-generation Jewish Americans.
Page Ref: 442

5) Explain the five revelations that led to Mormons being more widely accepted.
Page Ref: 449

6) How does Meidung help the Amish maintain their way of life?
Page Ref: 453–454

7) Discuss the role of ganja in the Rastafarian religion.
Page Ref: 457

8) Explain the role of reincarnation in the Hindu faith.
Page Ref: 463

9) Discuss the current religious controversies in the U.S.
Page Ref: 466

10) Apply the three sociological perspectives of an understanding of religion in U.S. society.
Page Ref: 468–470

Chapter 13 Women as a Minority Group

Multiple Choice Questions

1) Sexism as a term and concept has been a public concern since

    A) the Industrial Revolution.   B) World War II.

    C) the suffragette movement.   D) the 1960s.

Answer: D
Page Ref: 475

2) Freudian psychologists suggested that

    A) gender differences affected behavior.

    B) biological differences had no effect on behavior.

    C) all sex role behavior was learned.

    D) females were actually more aggressive than males.

Answer: A
Page Ref: 475

3) Who suggested that male genitalia influenced boys to be questing, aggressive, and outward-thrusting and that female genitalia directed girls to be concerned with boundaries, limits and "interiors"?

    A) Friedan   B) Hacker   C) Erikson   D) Myrdal

Answer: C
Page Ref: 475

4) Women possessed which of the following minority-group characteristics?

    A) ascribed status

    B) easily identifiable

    C) recognize their commonality with one another as victims of an ideology

    D) all of the above

Answer: D
Page Ref: 476

5) Congress gave women the right to vote in

    A) 1789.   B) 1865.   C) 1890.   D) 1919.

Answer: D
Page Ref: 478

6) Mead's study of the Arapesh, Mundugamor, and Tchambuli found

    A) evidence of consistent sex differences in behavior.

    B) cultural variance in male–female role behavior.

    C) greater male aggression in primitive societies.

    D) less male aggression in primitive societies.

Answer: B
Page Ref: 480

7) Socialization causes boys to have less _____ than girls.

    A) anxiety   B) impulsiveness

    C) explorative curiosity   D) self-reliance

Answer: A
Page Ref: 481

8) Which statement is most correct about television?

    A) It helps overcome sex stereotyping.

    B) It significantly improved its realistic portrayal of women.

    C) It continues to promote traditional sex stereotypes.

    D) It has no pattern of promoting sex stereotyping.

Answer: C
Page Ref: 482–483

9) What is often overlooked about traditional sex roles within many working–class families?

    A) their income needs

    B) Most wives have full-time jobs.

    C) Many are second-generation Americans.

    D) Women spend much time on household duties.

Answer: C
Page Ref: 484

10) Special concerns of minority women include

    A) involuntary sterilization.

    B) monolingual education and services.

    C) high infant and maternal mortality rates.

    D) poor housing.

    E) all of the above.

Answer: E
Page Ref: 486

11) Which statement is most correct about foreign-born women?

    A) Asians tend to have more egalitarian sex roles than Hispanics.

    B) Hispanics tend to have more egalitarian sex roles that Asians.

    C) Both Asians and Hispanics tend to have egalitarian sex roles.

    D) Neither Asians nor Hispanics tend to have egalitarian sex roles.

Answer: D
Page Ref: 485

12) In 1998, Ula Taylor found that black women

    A) prefer the term *womanism* over *feminism*.

    B) reject feminism.

    C) oppose self-empowerment.

    D) emphasize their femininity over their cultural identity.

Answer: A
Page Ref: 486

13) Sexual biases in schools

    A) continues to exist.

    B) has almost completely disappeared.

    C) is the worst it has ever been in the history of the U.S.

    D) all of the above

Answer: A
Page Ref: 488

14) In fields of study in college today, we find

    A) proportional representation of males and females in most areas.

    B) females outnumbering males in the sciences.

    C) males significantly outnumbering females in engineering and physical sciences.

    D) females outnumbering males in computer and informational sciences.

Answer: C
Page Ref: 489

15) Occupations overwhelmingly filled by women are often called _____ jobs.

    A) softie   B) pink collar

    C) throwaway   D) pedestal-protection

Answer: B
Page Ref: 491

16) The greatest increase in working women has been among

    A) young unmarried women.   B) married women with young children.

    C) mothers of grown children.   D) widows.

Answer: B
Page Ref: 490

17) The term "glass ceiling" refers to

    A) most women working in office buildings.

    B) the shattering of past limits on women's salaries.

    C) discrimination against female upward mobility.

    D) Affirmative Action opening new careers for women.

Answer: C
Page Ref: 492

18) The term "second shift" refers to

    A) women working at two different job locations.

    B) women as a second source of family income.

    C) working women also doing most household chores.

    D) all of the above.

Answer: C
Page Ref: 493

19) Which statement is correct?

    A) Women earn less than men in almost every occupation.

    B) Women earn the same as men in most occupations.

    C) Women earn more than men in half the occupations.

    D) Men earn less than women in sales and teaching.

Answer: A
Page Ref: 493

20) If educational levels are equal, which of the following statements is correct?

    A) Black women earn about the same as white women.

    B) Black women often work longer hours than white women.

    C) both A and B

    D) none of the above

Answer: C
Page Ref: 493

21) The term "mommy track" refers to the

    A) reality that most mothers also work at a paying job.

    B) desire of most working women to become mothers.

    C) choice working women make to put family ahead of career.

    D) none of the above

Answer: C
Page Ref: 493–494

22) The growing number of female-headed households living in poverty has led to the creation of the concept of

    A) feminization of poverty.   B) discrimination.

    C) unfair treatment of women.   D) none of the above.

Answer: A
Page Ref: 495

23) Public concern about sexual harassment began

    A) in the medieval period.   B) with the suffragette movement.

    C) with the civil rights movement.   D) in the mid-1970s.

Answer: D
Page Ref: 495

24) One year after the Hill–Thomas hearings, public opinion

    A) heavily favored Anita Hill over Clarence Thomas.

    B) heavily favored Clarence Thomas over Anita Hill.

    C) hardly believed the Senate Committee treated her fairly.

    D) was evenly divided whether to believe Hill or Thomas.

Answer: D
Page Ref: 496

25) Many state labor laws

    A) protect women from economic exploitation.

    B) restrict women's employment opportunities.

    C) restrict women's income potential.

    D) all of the above

Answer: D
Page Ref: 497

26) Which statement is most correct?

    A) Women are underrepresented in Congress but not in state legislatures.

    B) Women are underrepresented in state legislatures but not as mayors.

    C) Women are only underrepresented as governors of states.

    D) Women are underrepresented at all levels of government.

Answer: D
Page Ref: 498

27) Functionalists suggest gender-linked tasks became questioned after all but

    A) labor-saving home appliances.

    B) machines doing labor tasks requiring strength.

    C) increase in immigration.

    D) reduction in infant mortality rate.

Answer: C
Page Ref: 500-501

28) Conflict theorists suggest sexual equality or inequality has usually rested heavily upon

    A) the degree of industrialization in a society.

    B) women's economic contributions to the society.

    C) women achieving political power.

    D) the willingness of men to allow equality.

Answer: B
Page Ref: 502

29) Which of the following is <u>not</u> part of interactionist analysis?

    A) male advantages in maintaining sexual inequality

    B) cultural conditioning

    C) social definition

    D) internalized societal expectations

Answer: A
Page Ref: 503

30) Interactionists suggest we can overcome sexual biases and stereotypes through use of

    A) our education institutions.   B) the media.

    C) parent education.   D) all of the above

Answer: D
Page Ref: 503-504

True/False Questions

1) In 1944, Myrdal noted a parallel between the position of women and blacks in U.S. society.

Answer: TRUE
Page Ref: 476

2) Women were considered sexual property in settlement areas with a shortage of women.

Answer: TRUE
Page Ref: 476

3) The abolitionist movement attracted female activists who wanted to maintain the enslavement of blacks.

Answer: FALSE
Page Ref: 477

4) Numerous studies have identified no sex-specific differences in brain functioning.

Answer: FALSE
Page Ref: 480

5) Studies show mothers and fathers touch, handle, speak to, play with, and discipline children differently, depending on the child's sex.

Answer: TRUE
Page Ref: 481

6) Flagrant sexism and sex role stereotyping abound in all forms of the media.

Answer: TRUE
Page Ref: 482

7) Kitano suggests that the personal dissatisfaction among second-generation Japanese American women in their expected female roles may be a primary reason that their acculturation was more rapid and their out-group-marriage rate greater than those of other Asian American women.

Answer: TRUE
Page Ref: 485

8) Low-income African American women easily identified with the feminist movement because many of its needs echoed their own needs.

Answer: FALSE
Page Ref: 485

9) In 1911, a Harvard professor argued that attempting to teach women would "weaken the intellect of the teacher."

Answer: TRUE
Page Ref: 487

10) Women typically earn 63–69 cents for every dollar earned by men.

Answer: TRUE
Page Ref: 493

Essay Questions

1) Discuss the evolution of the women's movement in the U.S.
Page Ref: 476

2) In what areas were women denied equal rights?
Page Ref: 477

3) Beside physical and reproductive organ differences, what other biological differences exist between men and women?
Page Ref: 480

4) Discuss the role of socialization in developing sex role behavior.
Page Ref: 480

5) Discuss the media's role in stereotyping and discriminating against women.
Page Ref: 482–483

6) Explain the concept of "role entrapment."
Page Ref: 484

7) What did your author mean when he said that women are at a double disadvantage in our society?
Page Ref: 486

8) Discuss the concept of sexual harassment and its occurrence in the military and workplace.
Page Ref: 497

9) What problems of sexism are institutionalized in law?
Page Ref: 497

10) Discuss the functionalist's, conflict theorist's, and interactionist's explanation for male-dominance in the U.S.
Page Ref: 500–504

Chapter 14 The Ever-Changing U.S. Mosaic

Multiple Choice Questions

1) In today's world an immigrant group can maintain contact with the country of origin through

    A) airmail.   B) telecommunications.

    C) rapid transportation.   D) all of the above.

Answer: D
Page Ref: 510

2) The three-generation hypothesis suggests

    A) it usually takes three generations to complete the assimilation process.

    B) religious intermarriage occurs by the third generation.

    C) the third generation rediscovers its ethnicity.

    D) all of the above.

Answer: C
Page Ref: 512

3) Abramson and others criticize the three-generation hypothesis because it

    A) ignores diversity of region, social structure, and people.

    B) cannot be tested.

    C) ignores racial groups.

    D) requires three generations of time before analysis.

Answer: A
Page Ref: 512

4) According to Hansen, the process of assimilation is

    A) dialectical.   B) one way.

    C) permanent.   D) none of the above.

Answer: A
Page Ref: 512

5) Ethnic identity is

    A) an ascribed attribute.

    B) found only among those living in ethnic communities.

    C) not found among any racial groups.

    D) a creation of a pluralistic U.S. society.

Answer: D
Page Ref: 521

6) The Lieberson and Waters study of geographic concentrations of ethnic groups found

    A) no link between ethnicity and changing spatial patterns.

    B) a link between ethnic group size and location.

    C) no link between time living in the U.S. and geographic dispersal.

    D) a link between Asian and Hispanic avoidance of neighboring communities.

Answer: B
Page Ref: 517

7) According to Gans, symbolic ethnicity refers to

    A) taken-for-granted everyday realities.

    B) private observances such as foods, rituals, ethnic home objects.

    C) public displays such as marching in ethnic parades.

    D) both B and C.

Answer: D
Page Ref: 521

8) In his ecological model of Chicago's growth and development, Robert Park (1926) noted the linkage between social mobility and

    A) family commitment.   B) spatial mobility.

    C) popularity.   D) all of the above.

Answer: B
Page Ref: 517

9) According to Alba, which of the following helps sustain a strong sense of ethnic identity?

    A) ethnic neighborhoods

    B) ethnic organizations

    C) population numbers similar to the majority group

    D) both A and B

Answer: D
Page Ref: 521

10) The 9.1 million immigrants arriving in the U.S. in the 1990s is

    A) the second highest decade total.

    B) the highest decade total.

    C) a slight decrease from the 1960s.

    D) probably the last decade Europeans will dominate.

Answer: B
Page Ref: 524

11) Studies show that

    A) immigrants do not take jobs away from American workers.

    B) immigrants do not adversely affect the earnings of other groups.

    C) immigrants do not a financial burden on services.

    D) all of the above

Answer: D
Page Ref: 525

12) Public funding for bilingual education began in 1968, when Congress passed the

    A) Bilingual Education Act.   B) Equal Opportunity Act.

    C) Educational Accessibility Act.   D) none of the above

Answer: A
Page Ref: 528

13) English as a Second Language programs have expanded to include _____ languages.

    A) 3.   B) 45.   C) 106.   D) 125

Answer: D
Page Ref: 529

14) Today, most illegal aliens are coming from

    A) Canada.   B) Colombia.   C) Puerto Rico.   D) Mexico.

Answer: D
Page Ref: 527

15) Federal legislation in 1988 set a normal limit for bilingual education of _____ years.

    A) two   B) three   C) four   D) five

Answer: B
Page Ref: 530

16) Recent government studies reveal that bilingual education

   A) has little value in aiding academic success.

   B) helps foreign-born students succeed academically.

   C) is comparable in success rates to immersion programs.

   D) both B and C

Answer: D
Page Ref: 530

17) Two national studies found that almost all Hispanic parents

   A) emphasize Spanish over English for their children.

   B) hold back their children's learning English.

   C) stress English as critically important.

   D) are very casual about their children learning English.

Answer: C
Page Ref: 533

18) Fostering separation instead of a cohesive society is called

   A) language exclusion.   B) ethnic tribalism.

   C) selective relations.   D) all of the above.

Answer: B
Page Ref: 531

19) By 2004, how many states had passed English-only legislation?

   A) 4   B) 9   C) 14   D) 27

Answer: D
Page Ref: 531

20) New multiculturists advocate "minority nationalism" and

   A) "collaborative pluralism."   B) "freedom of movement."

   C) "separatis pluralism."   D) both A and B.

Answer: C
Page Ref: 533

21) Census Bureau projections for 2050 include

    A) Hispanics becoming the largest minority group.

    B) blacks decreasing in their proportion of the population.

    C) Asians remaining at the present percentage.

    D) all of the above.

    Answer: A
    Page Ref: 536

22) Which pro–immigration advocate argues that multiculturalism undermines the assimilation ethic?

    A) Karl Marx   B) Herbert Gans

    C) S. I. Hayakawa   D) John J. Miller

    Answer: D
    Page Ref: 534

23) Which of the following countries does not encourage cultural diversity?

    A) France   B) England

    C) Australia   D) all of the above

    Answer: A
    Page Ref: 533

24) One limitation of census projections is

    A) the population rarely stays stagnant.

    B) that it assumes that conditions worldwide will remain constant.

    C) does not account for birth rates.

    D) does not account for medical advances.

    Answer: B
    Page Ref: 537

25) There is great concern that the Census Bureau projections will fall victim to the

    A) Dillingham Flaw.   B) Calculation Error Debate.

    C) Regression Toward the Mean.   D) none of the above

    Answer: A
    Page Ref: 537

26) With increased immigration comes the issue of

    A) interethnic marriages.   B) higher divorce rates.

    C) higher birth rates.   D) mixed identity beliefs.

Answer: A
Page Ref: 537

27) According to recent public–opinion polls, Americans have _____ opinions about immigration.

    A) strictly posititve   B) undeniably negative

    C) mixed   D) indifferent

Answer: C
Page Ref: 526

28) Official estimates place the number of undocumented aliens currently living in the United States at

    A) 1 million.   B) 3 million.   C) 6 million.   D) 10 million.

Answer: C
Page Ref: 527

29) In 2003, which country had the largest number of undocumented aliens in the U.S.?

    A) Mexico   B) Germany   C) South Africa   D) Asia

Answer: A
Page Ref: 527

30) Current migration patterns offer clues about _____ of future Americans.

    A) the political party domination   B) the legal implications of citizenship

    C) the religious preferences   D) none of the above

Answer: C
Page Ref: 539

True/False Questions

1) Ethnocentric values prompted the natural development of ingroup loyalty and outgroup hostility among both indigenous and migrant groups.

Answer: TRUE
Page Ref: 509

2) All immigrants begin at the bottom of the socioeconomic ladder.

Answer: FALSE
Page Ref: 509

3) Because Japan ranks among the leading capitalist nations, its immigrants enjoy a status of "honorary whites."

Answer: TRUE
Page Ref: 511

4) Thomas Sowell argued that cultural characteristics that either mesh or clash with the dominant cultural values determine a group's upward mobility.

Answer: TRUE
Page Ref: 513

5) New immigrants tend to shed their "cultural baggage" and choose to assimilate in their new home.

Answer: FALSE
Page Ref: 513

6) Transnationalism refers to sustained ties of persons, networks, and organizations across national borders.

Answer: TRUE
Page Ref: 513

7) Social wealth refers to the power that some new immigrants have in the U.S.

Answer: FALSE
Page Ref: 514

8) High intermarriage rates not only have lessened the intergenerational transmission of the distinctive cultural traits but also have diversified the ethnic ancestry of third- and fourth-generation European Americans.

Answer: TRUE
Page Ref: 521

9) Echoing xenophobic fears of earlier generations, immigration opponents worry that U.S. citizens will lose control of the country to foreigners.

Answer: TRUE
Page Ref: 524

10) The nation's unstable birthrate means that immigrants cannot account for a larger share of population growth than in previous years.

Answer: FALSE
Page Ref: 524

Essay Questions

1) Explain why the country of origin is a factor in understanding immigrant interaction patterns.
Page Ref: 509

2) Discuss the divergent views about the three-generation hypothesis.
Page Ref: 512–513

3) Explain the concept of transnationalism.
Page Ref: 513

4) Discuss the value of symbolic ethnicity in people's lives and its relationship to the everyday ethnicity of newer Americans.
Page Ref: 521

5) Discuss Alejandro Portes' and Min Zhou's theory of segmented assimilation.
Page Ref: 514

6) Discuss the claims and counterclaims about the impact of illegal aliens on American society.
Page Ref: 522–523

7) Discuss the controversy surrounding bilingual education.
Page Ref: 528

8) Discuss the evolving positions of the multiculturalists and offer your analytical commentary.
Page Ref: 533

9) What minority- and majority-response patterns have you witnessed throughout the discussion of immigration in the text?
Page Ref: 522–536

10) Discuss your views of what America might be like in the mid–twenty-first century if Census Bureau projections become true.
Page Ref: 623

Teaching Tips for First-time Instructors and Adjunct Professors

Teaching Tips Contents

1. How to be an Effective Teacher
Seven principles of good teaching practice
Tips for Thriving: Creating an Inclusive Classroom

2. Today's Undergraduate Students
Traditional students
Nontraditional students
Emerging influences
What students want from college professors
Tips for Thriving: Be a "Facilitator of Learning"

3. Planning Your Course
Constructing the syllabus
Problems to avoid
Tips for Thriving: Visual Quality

4. Your First Class
Seven goals for a successful first meeting
Tips for Thriving: An Icebreaker

5. Strategies for Teaching and Learning
Getting participation through active learning
Team learning
Tips for Thriving: Active Learning and Lecturing

6. Grading and Assessment Techniques
Philosophy of grading
Criterion grading
Tips for Thriving: Result Feedback

7. Using Technology
Advice on using the web in small steps
Tips for Thriving: Using Videos

8. Managing Problem Situations
Cheating
Unmotivated students
Credibility problems
Tips for Thriving: Discipline

9. Surviving When You're Not Prepared
Contingency plans

10. Improving Your Performance
Self evaluation
Tips for Thriving: Video-Recording Your Class

1   How to be an Effective Teacher

(Adapted from Royse, *Teaching Tips for College and University Instructors: A Practical Guide*, published by Allyn & Bacon, Boston, MA, ©2001, by Pearson Education)

A look at 50 years of research "on the way teachers teach and learners learn" reveals seven broad principles of good teaching practice (Chickering and Gamson, 1987).

1. Frequent student-faculty contact: Faculty who are concerned about their students and their progress and who are perceived to be easy to talk to, serve to motivate and keep students involved. Things you can do to apply this principle:
- ✓ Attend events sponsored by students.
- ✓ Serve as a mentor or advisor to students.
- ✓ Keep "open" or "drop-in" office hours.

2. The encouragement of cooperation among students: There is a wealth of research indicating that students benefit from the use of small group and peer learning instructional approaches. Things you can do to apply this principle:
- ✓ Have students share in class their interests and backgrounds.
- ✓ Create small groups to work on projects together.
- ✓ Encourage students to study together.

3. Active learning techniques: Students don't learn much by sitting in the classroom listening; they must talk about what they are learning, write about it, relate to it, and apply it to their lives. Things you can do to apply this principle:
- ✓ Give students actual problems or situations to analyze.
- ✓ Use role-playing, simulations or hands-on experiments.
- ✓ Encourage students to challenge ideas brought into class.

4. Prompt feedback: Learning theory research has consistently shown that the quicker the feedback, the greater the learning. Things you can do to apply this principle:
- ✓ Return quizzes and exams by the next class meeting.
- ✓ Return homework within one week.
- ✓ Provide students with detailed comments on their written papers.

5. Emphasize time on task: This principle refers to the amount of actual involvement with the material being studied and applies, obviously, to the way the instructor uses classroom instructional time. Faculty need good time-management skills. Things you can do to apply this principle:
- ✓ Require students who miss classes to make up lost work.
- ✓ Require students to rehearse before making oral presentations.
- ✓ Don't let class breaks stretch out too long.

6. Communicating high expectations: The key here is not to make the course impossibly difficult, but to have goals that can be attained as long as individual learners stretch and work hard, going beyond what they already know. Things you can do to apply this principle:
- ✓ Communicate your expectations orally and in writing at the beginning of the course.
- ✓ Explain the penalties for students who turn work in late.
- ✓ Identify excellent work by students; display exemplars if possible.

7. Respecting diverse talents and ways of learning: Within any classroom there will be students who have latent talents and some with skills and abilities far beyond any that you might imagine. Understanding your students as individuals and showing regard for their unique talents is "likely to facilitate student growth and development in every sphere – academic, social, personal, and vocational" (Sorcinelli, 1991, p.21). Things you can do to apply this principle:

✓ Use diverse teaching approaches.
✓ Allow students some choice of readings and assignments.
✓ Try to find out students' backgrounds and interests.

 Tips for Thriving: Creating an Inclusive Classroom

How do you model an open, accepting attitude within your classroom where students will feel it is safe to engage in give-and-take discussions? Firstly, view students as individuals instead of representatives of separate and distinct groups. Cultivate a climate that is respectful of diverse viewpoints, and don't allow ridicule, defamatory or hurtful remarks. Try to encourage everyone in the class to participate, and be alert to showing favoritism.

2   Today's Undergraduate Students

(Adapted from: Lyons et al, *The Adjunct Professor's Guide to Success*, published by Allyn & Bacon, Boston, MA, ©1999, by Pearson Education)

Total enrollment in all forms of higher education has increased over 65% in the last thirty years. Much of this increase was among part-time students who now comprise over 70% of total college enrollment. The number of "nontraditional" students, typically defined as 25 years of age or older, has been growing more rapidly than the number of "traditional" students, those under 25 years of age. Though there is a great deal of common ground between students of any age, there are some key differences between younger and older students.

Traditional students: Much more than in previous generations, traditional students are the products of dysfunctional families and have had a less effective primary and secondary education. Traditional students have been conditioned by the aftermath of high-profile ethical scandals (such as Watergate), creating a mindset of cynicism and lack of respect for authority figures – including college professors. Students of this generation are quick to proclaim their "rights". Many of today's students perceive professors as service providers, class attendance as a matter of individual choice, and grades as "pay" to which they are entitled for meeting standards they perceive as reasonable.

Nontraditional students: Many older students are attending college after a long lay-off, frequently doubting their ability to succeed. The other time-consuming challenges in their lives – children, work, caring for aging parents – often prevent adequate preparation for class or contribute to frequent absences. While traditional students demand their "rights," many older students won't ask for the smallest extra consideration (e.g., to turn a project in a few days late). Most older students learn best by doing, by applying the theory of the textbook to the rich set of experiences they have accumulated over the years.

Emerging influences: Today, a fourth of all undergraduate students are members of minority groups. Obviously, ethnicity, language, religion, culture, and sexual orientation are each significant issues to which a professor should be sensitive. The successful professor sees these differences as an opportunity rather than a threat to learning.

 Tips for Thriving: Be a "Facilitator of Learning"

Be energized by students who "don't get it" rather than judgmental of their shortcomings. View yourself as a "facilitator of learning" rather than a "sage on a stage."

What students want from college professors: While each student subgroup has particular characteristics that affect the dynamics of a college learning environment, students consistently need the following from their college instructors:

- ✓ Consistently communicated expectations of student performance that are reasonable in quantity and quality
- ✓ Sensitivity to the diverse demands on students and reasonable flexibility in accommodating them
- ✓ Effective use of classroom time
- ✓ A classroom environment that includes humor and spontaneity
- ✓ Examinations that address issues properly covered in class and are appropriate to the level of the majority of the students in the class
- ✓ Consistently positive treatment of individual students

The new paradigm of "colleges and universities as service providers to consumer-oriented students" is now firmly entrenched. The successful professor will do well to embrace it.

3   Planning Your Course

(Adapted from Royse, *Teaching Tips for College and University Instructors: A Practical Guide*, published by Allyn & Bacon, Boston, MA, ©2001, by Pearson Education)

Constructing the syllabus: The syllabus should clearly communicate course objectives, assignments, required readings, and grading policies. Think of the syllabus as a stand-alone document. Those students who miss the first or second meeting of a class should be able to learn most of what they need to know about the requirements of the course from reading the syllabus. Start by collecting syllabi from colleagues who have recently taught the course you will be teaching and look for common threads and themes.

Problems to avoid: One mistake commonly made by educators teaching a course for the first time is that they may have rich and intricate visions of how they want students to demonstrate comprehension and synthesis of the material, but they somehow fail to convey this information to those enrolled. Check your syllabus to make sure your expectations have been fully articulated. Be very specific. Avoid vaguely worded instructions:

Instruction	Students may interpret as:
"Write a short paper."	Write a paragraph.
	Write half a page.
	Type a two-page paper.
"Keep a log of your experiences."	Make daily entries.
	Make an entry when the spirit moves me.
	At the end of term, record what I recall.
"Obtain an article from the library."	Any magazine article.
	An article from a professional journal.
	A column from a newsletter.

 Tips for Thriving: Visual Quality

Students today are highly visual learners, so you should give special emphasis to the visual quality of the materials you provide to students. Incorporate graphics into your syllabus and other handouts. Color-code your materials so material for different sections of the course are on different colored papers. Such visuals are likely to create a perception among students that you are contemporary.

(Adapted from: Lyons et al, *The Adjunct Professor's Guide to Success*, published by Allyn & Bacon, Boston, MA, ©1999, by Pearson Education)

Success in achieving a great start is almost always directly attributable to the quality and quantity of planning that has been invested by the course professor. If the first meeting of your class is to be successful, you should strive to achieve seven distinct goals.

Create a Positive First Impression: Renowned communications consultant Roger Ailes (1996) claims you have fewer than 10 seconds to create a positive image of yourself. Students are greatly influenced by the visual component; therefore you must look the part of the professional professor. Dress as you would for a professional job interview. Greet each student entering the room. Be approachable and genuine.

Introduce Yourself Effectively: Communicate to students who you are and why you are credible as the teacher of the course. Seek to establish your approachability by "building common ground," such as stating your understanding of students' hectic lifestyles or their common preconceptions toward the subject matter.

Clarify the Goals and Expectations: Make an acetate transparency of each page of the syllabus for display on an overhead projector and using a cover sheet, expose each section as you explain it. Provide clarification and elicit questions.

Conduct an Activity that Introduces Students to Each Other: Students' chances of being able to complete a course effectively is enhanced if each comes to perceive the classmates as a "support network." The small amount of time you invest in an icebreaker will help create a positive classroom atmosphere and pay additional dividends throughout the term.

 Tips for Thriving: Icebreaker

The following activity allows students to get acquainted, exchange opinions, and consider new ideas, values or solutions to problems. It's a great way to promote self-disclosure or an active exchange of viewpoints.

Procedure

1. Give students one or more Post-it™ notes
2. Ask them to write on their note(s) one of the following:
   a. A *value* they hold
   b. An *experience* they have had recently
   c. A *creative idea* or solution to a problem you have posed
   d. A *question* they have about the subject matter of the class
   e. An *opinion* they hold about a topic of your choosing
   f. A *fact* about themselves or the subject matter of the class
3. Ask students to stick the note(s) on their clothing and circulate around the room reading each other's notes.
4. Next, have students mingle once again and negotiate a trade of Post-it™ notes with one another. The trade should be based on a desire to possess a particular value, experience, idea, question, opinion or fact for a short period of time. Set the rule that all trades have to be two-way. Encourage students to make as many trades as they like.
5. Reconvene the class and ask students to share what trades they made and why. (e.g., "I traded for a note that Sally had stating that she has traveled to Eastern Europe. I would really like to travel there because I have ancestors from Hungary and the Ukraine.")

(Adapted from: Silverman, *Active Learning: 101 Strategies to Teach Any Subject*, published by Allyn & Bacon, Boston, MA, ©1996, by Pearson Education).

Learn Students' Names: A student who is regularly addressed by name feels more valued, is invested more effectively in classroom discussion, and will approach the professor with questions and concerns.

Whet Students' Appetite for the Course Material: The textbook adopted for the course is critical to your success. Your first meeting should include a review of its approach, features, and sequencing. Explain to students what percentage of class tests will be derived from material from the textbook.

Reassure Students of the Value of the Course: At the close of your first meeting reassure students that the course will be a valuable learning experience and a wise investment of their time. Review the reasons why the course is a good investment: important and relevant content, interesting classmates, and a dynamic classroom environment.

5   Strategies for Teaching and Learning

(Adapted from: Silverman, *Active Learning: 101 Strategies to Teach Any Subject,* published by Allyn & Bacon, Boston, MA, ©1996, by Pearson Education)

Getting participation through active learning: To learn something well, it helps to hear it, see it, ask questions about it, and discuss it with others. What makes learning "active"? When learning is active, students do most of the work: they use their brains to study ideas, solve problems, and apply what they learn. Active learning is fast-paced, fun, supportive, and personally engaging. Active learning cannot occur without student participation, so there are various ways to structure discussion and obtain responses from students at any time during a class. Here are ten methods to get participation at any time:

1. **Open discussion**. Ask a question and open it up to the entire class without further structuring.
2. **Response cards**. Pass out index cards and request anonymous answers to your questions.
3. **Polling**. Design a short survey that is filled out and tallied on the spot.
4. **Subgroup discussion**. Break students into subgroups of three or more to share and record information.
5. **Learning partners**. Have students work on tasks with the student sitting next to them.
6. **Whips**. Go around the group and obtain short responses to key questions – invite students to pass if they wish.
7. **Panels**. Invite a small number of students to present their views in front of the class.
8. **Fishbowl**. Ask a portion of the class to form a discussion circle and have the remaining students form a listening circle around them. Bring new groups into the inner circle to continue the discussion.
9. **Games**. Use a fun exercise or quiz game to elicit students' ideas, knowledge, or skill.
10. **Calling on the next speaker**. Ask students to raise their hands when they want to share their views and ask the current speaker to choose the next speaker.

(Adapted from Royse, *Teaching Tips for College and University Instructors: A Practical Guide*, published by Allyn & Bacon, Boston, MA, ©2001, by Pearson Education)

Team learning: The essential features of this small group learning approach, developed originally for use in large college classrooms are (1) relatively permanent heterogeneous task groups; (2) grading based on a combination of individual performance, group performance, and peer evaluation; (3) organization of the course so that the majority of class time is spent on small group activities; (4) a six-step instructional process similar to the following model:

1. Individual study of material outside of the class is assigned.
2. Individual testing is used (multiple choice questions over homework at the beginning of class)
3. Groups discuss their answers and then are given a group test of the same items. They then get immediate feedback (answers).
4. Groups may prepare written appeals of items.

5. Feedback is given from instructor.
6. An application-oriented activity is assigned (e.g. a problem to be solved requiring input from all group members).

If you plan to use team learning in your class, inform students at the beginning of the course of your intentions to do so and explain the benefits of small group learning. Foster group cohesion by sitting groups together and letting them choose "identities" such as a team name or slogan. You will need to structure and supervise the groups and ensure that the projects build on newly acquired learning. Make the projects realistic and interesting and ensure that they are adequately structured so that each member's contribution is 25 percent. Students should be given criteria by which they can assess and evaluate the contributions of their peers on a project-by-project basis (Michaelsen, 1994).

 Tips for Thriving: Active Learning and Lecturing

Lecturing is one of the most time-honored teaching methods, but does it have a place in an active learning environment? There are times when lecturing can be effective. Think about the following when planning a lecture:

Build Interest: Capture your students' attention by leading off with an anecdote or cartoon.
Maximize Understanding and Retention: Use brief handouts and demonstrations as a visual backup to enable your students to see as well as hear.
Involve Students during the Lecture: Interrupt the lecture occasionally to challenge students to answer spot quiz questions.
Reinforce the Lecture: Give students a self-scoring review test at the end of the lecture.

6   Grading and Assessment Techniques

(Adapted from Wankat, *The Effective, Efficient Professor: Teaching, Scholarship and Service*, published by Allyn & Bacon, Boston, MA, ©2002, by Pearson Education)

Philosophy of grading: Develop your own philosophy of grading by picturing in your mind the performance of typical A students, B students and so on. Try different grading methods until you find one that fits your philosophy and is reasonably fair. Always look closely at students on grade borders – take into account personal factors if the group is small. Be consistent with or slightly more generous than the procedure outlined in your syllabus.

Criterion grading: Professor Philip Wankat writes: "I currently use a form of criterion grading for my sophomore and junior courses. I list the scores in the syllabus that will guarantee the students As, Bs and so forth. For example, a score of 85 to 100 guarantees an A; 75 to 85, a B; 65 to 75, a C; and 55 to 65, a D. If half the class gets above 85% they all get an A. This reduces competition and allows students to work together and help each other. The standard grade gives students something to aim for and tells them exactly what their grade is at any time. For students whose net scores are close to the borders at the end of the course, I look at other factors before deciding a final grade such as attendance."

 Tips for Thriving: Result Feedback

As stated earlier, feedback on results is the most effective of motivating factors. Anxious students are especially hungry for positive feedback. You can quickly and easily provide it by simply writing "Great job!" on the answer sheets or tests. For students who didn't perform well, a brief note such as "I'd love to talk with you at the end of class" can be especially reassuring. The key is to be proactive and maintain high standards, while requiring students to retain ownership of their success.

7   <u>Using Technology</u>

(Adapted from: Sanders, *Creating Learning-Centered Courses for the World Wide Web*, published by Allyn & Bacon, Boston, MA, ©2001, by Pearson Education)

The Web as a source of teaching and learning has generated a great deal of excitement and hyperbole. The Web is neither a panacea nor a demon, but it can be a valuable tool. Among the many misunderstandings about the use of Web pages for teaching and learning is a view that such efforts must encompass an entire course. Like any other tool in a course (e.g. lectures, discussions, films, or field trips) online material can be incorporated to enhance the learning experience.

The best way to start using the Web in a course is with small steps. Developing a single lesson or assignment, a syllabus, or a few well-chosen links makes more sense than trying to develop a whole course without sufficient support or experience. Testing Web materials with a class that regularly meets face-to-face helps a faculty member gauge how well a lesson using the Web works. Making adjustments within the context of a traditional class helps fine-tune Web lessons that may be offered in distance education without face-to-face interaction.

 Tips for Thriving: Using Videos

Generally a videotape should not exceed half and hour in length. Always preview a video before showing it to ensure the content, language, and complexity are appropriate for your students. Include major videos on your syllabus to encourage attendance and integrate them into the context of the course. Plan to evaluate students' retention of the concepts on exams or through reports. Avoid reinforcing the common student perception that watching a video is a time-filler.

By beginning with good practices in learning, we ask not how the new technology can help us do a better job of getting students to learn, but rather we ask how good pedagogy be better implemented with the new technology.

8   <u>Managing Problem Situations</u>

(Adapted from Wankat, *The Effective, Efficient Professor: Teaching, Scholarship and Service*, published by Allyn & Bacon, Boston, MA, ©2002, by Pearson Education)

Cheating: Cheating is one behavior that should not be tolerated. Tolerating cheating tends to make it worse. Prevention of cheating is much more effective than trying to cure it once it has occurred. A professor can prevent cheating by:

- Creating rapport with students
- Gaining a reputation for giving fair tests
- Giving clear instructions and guidelines before, during, and after tests
- Educating students on the ethics of plagiarism
- Requiring periodic progress reports and outlines before a paper is due

Try to develop exams that are perceived as fair and secure by students. Often, the accusation that certain questions were tricky is valid as it relates to ambiguous language and trivial material. Ask your mentor or an experienced instructor to closely review the final draft of your first few exams for these factors.

Tips for Thriving: Discipline

One effective method for dealing with some discipline problems is to ask the class for feedback (Angelo & Cross, 1993) In a one-minute quiz, ask the students, "What can I do to help you learn?" Collate the responses and present them to the class. If behavior such as excessive talking appears in some responses (e.g. "Tell people to shut up") this gives you the backing to ask students to be quiet. Use of properly channeled peer pressure is often effective in controlling undesired behavior

(Adapted from Royse, *Teaching Tips for College and University Instructors: A Practical Guide*, published by Allyn & Bacon, Boston, MA, ©2001, by Pearson Education)

Unmotivated Students: There are numerous reasons why students may not be motivated. The "required course" scenario is a likely explanation – although politics in colonial America is your life's work, it is safe to assume that not everyone will share your enthusiasm. There are also personal reasons such as a death of a loved one or depression. Whenever you detect a pattern that you assume to be due to lack of motivation (e.g. missing classes, not handing assignments in on time, non-participation in class), arrange a time to have the student meet with you outside the classroom. Candidly express your concerns and then listen.

Motivating students is part of the faculty members' job. To increase motivation professors should: show enthusiasm for the topic; use various media and methods to present material; use humor in the classroom; employ activities that encourage active learning; and give frequent, positive feedback.

(Adapted from Baiocco/Waters, *Successful College Teaching*, published by Allyn & Bacon, Boston, MA, ©1998, by Pearson Education)

Credibility Problems. If you are an inexperienced instructor you may have problems with students not taking you seriously. At the first class meeting articulate clear rules of classroom decorum and comport yourself with dignity and respect for students. Try to exude that you are in charge and are the "authority" and avoid trying to pose as the students' friend.

9 Surviving When You're Not Prepared

(Adapted from: Lyons et al, *The Adjunct Professor's Guide to Success*, published by Allyn & Bacon, Boston, MA, ©1999, by Pearson Education)

Despite your thorough course planning, your concern for students, and commitment to the institution, situations will arise – illness, family emergencies – that prevent you from being fully prepared for every class meeting. Most students will excuse one flawed performance during a term, but try to develop contingency plans you can employ on short notice. These might include:

- Recruiting a guest speaker from your circle of colleagues to deliver a presentation that might interest your students.
- Conducting a carousel brainstorming activity, in which a course issue is examined from several perspectives. Divide the students in to groups to identify facts appropriate to each perspective. For example, you might want to do a SWOT analysis (Strengths, Weaknesses, Opportunities, Threats) on a particular organization or public figure.
- Dividing the class into groups of three or four and asking them to develop several questions that would be appropriate for inclusion on your next exam.
- Identify a video at your local rental store that embellishes material from the course.
- Assign students roles (e.g. press, governmental figures, etc.), and conduct a focused analysis of a late-breaking news story related to your course.
- Divide students into groups to work on an assigned course project or upcoming exam.
- As a last resort, admit your inability to prepare a class and allow students input into formulating a strategy for best utilizing class time.

In each case, the key is to shift the initial attention away from yourself (to permit you to gather your thoughts) and onto an activity that engages students in a new and significant way.

10   Improving Your Performance

(Adapted from: Lyons et al, *The Adjunct Professor's Guide to Success*, published by Allyn & Bacon, Boston, MA, ©1999, by Pearson Education)

The instructor who regularly engages in systematic self-evaluation will unquestionably derive greater reward from the formal methods of evaluation commonly employed by colleges and universities. One method for providing structure to an ongoing system of self-evaluation is to keep a journal of reflections on your teaching experiences. Regularly invest 15 or 20 introspective minutes following each class meeting to focus especially on the strategies and events in class that you feel could be improved. Committing your thoughts and emotions enables you to develop more effective habits, build confidence in your teaching performance, and make more effective comparisons later. The following questions will help guide self-assessment:

> *How do I typically begin the class?*
> *Where/How do I position myself in the class?*
> *How do I move in the classroom?*
> *Where are my eyes usually focused?*
> *Do I facilitate students' visual processing of course material?*
> *Do I change the speed, volume, energy, and tone of my voice?*
> *How do I ask questions of students?*
> *How often, and when, do I smile or laugh in class?*
> *How do I react when students are inattentive?*
> *How do I react when students disagree or challenge what I say?*
> *How do I typically end a class?*

 Tips for Thriving: Video-Recording Your Class

In recent years a wide range if professionals have markedly improved their job performance by employing video recorders in their preparation efforts. As an instructor, an effective method might be to ask your mentor or another colleague to tape a 10 to 15 minute mini-lesson then to debrief it using the assessment questions above. Critiquing a videotaped session provides objectivity and is therefore more likely to effect change. Involving a colleague as an informal coach will enable you to gain from their experience and perspective and will reduce the chances of your engaging in self-depreciation.

References

Ailes, R. (1996) *You are the message: Getting what you want by being who you are.* New York: Doubleday.
Chickering, A.W., & Gamson, Z.F. (1987) Seven principles for good practice in undergraduate education. AAHE Bulletin, 39, 3-7.
Michaelson, L.K. (1994). Team Learning: Making a case for the small-group option. In K.W. Prichard & R.M. Sawyer (Eds.), *Handbook of college teaching.* Westport, CT: Greenwood Press.
Sorcinelli, M.D. (1991). Research findings on the seven principles. In A.W. Chickering & Z. Gamson (eds.), *Applying the seven principles of good practice in undergraduate education.* New Directions for Teaching and Learning #47. San Francisco: Jossey-Bass.

NOTES

NOTES

NOTES

NOTES

NOTES

NOTES

NOTES

NOTES